CW00767708

A WEAVING
OF PEACE

ABOUT THE AUTHOR

Susan Hardwick is an Anglican priest in Coventry Diocese. She trained for the ordained ministry at Queen's College, Birmingham (1982-5), since when she has worked for the Coventry Diocese in various areas of ministry. Susan Hardwick was priested in 1994 at Coventry Cathedral; she is married to an Anglican priest and has two grown-up children.

A WEAVING
OF PEACE

Susan Hardwick

Foreword by
Gerard W. Hughes SJ

Kevin
Mayhew

First published in 1996 by
KEVIN MAYHEW LTD
Rattlesden
Bury St Edmunds
Suffolk IP30 0SZ

0 1 2 3 4 5 6 7 8 9

ISBN 0 86209 854 8
Catalogue No 1500058

Typesetting by Louise Hill
Printed and bound in Great Britain.

FOREWORD

Spirituality has become popular today. Our need of spirituality is acknowledged, not only in church sacristies and vestries, but also in business boardrooms. While this interest is to be welcomed, it also has its dangers. Has spirituality become the latest object of consumerism, an interest which will enhance the feel-good factor of material affluence?

A Weaving of Peace is a sobering reminder of the nature of Christian spirituality, that it must never become an escape from the horrors and brutishness of human life, but should help us to face and engage with these realities, not only in others, but most of all in ourselves, with an unconquerable hope, even when everything seems hopeless.

The author starts with Auschwitz and the problems it raises for every human being – 'About a God who cannot/will not intervene. About the efficacy of prayer. About the basic goodness/evil in humankind: which dominates? About individual responsibility. About forgiveness and its limits – even for God'. (p. 85)

In Jerusalem the author ponders the questions of human brokenness, rejection, suffering, healing, reconciliation, re-creation in the light of Christ's suffering, death and resurrection, and finds that even in places of despair and death there is also the continuous breaking through of new life.

Although the subject matter is heavy, Susan Hardwick's style is light and gentle. She is constantly finding connections between all that she sees and all that she believes as a Christian. This, I think, is the strength of the book, for it prompts us to make our own connections between what happened two thousand years ago in Jerusalem, what happened in this century in Auschwitz, and what is happening in each of us now.

In Jerusalem the author met Fr Bruno Hussar, born of Jewish parents, brought up in Egypt with Muslims, now working as a Dominican priest in Israel. He considers himself to be both Jew, Muslim and Christian. He founded Neve Shalom, a community where Palestinians and Jews, Muslims and Christians, live and work together. He said to Susan, 'There is a mystical connection between people here and now, and Jesus'. This book explores that statement. I thank Susan Hardwick for the privilege of reading it in manuscript and I commend it to all who long to be able to hope, even when everything seems hopeless.

GERARD W. HUGHES SJ

DEDICATION

So many people to appreciate; here are some of them.

Coventry Diocese, where I am privileged to work, and which allowed me the Sabbatical during which much of this book was written.

The two who acted as supervisor and advisor and who generously shared their time, thinking, books, suggestions and wisdom, and who helped me initially to rein my cosmic-ranging thoughts into some sort of discipline and order: any theological errors are mine, not theirs.

Those whom I have met on my journeying and who, with open hands and hearts, gave in such a variety of ways.

But especially Gerard Hughes, who has been my guide and companion on the Way for a number of years and from whom I have learned, and continue to learn, so much about so much; who, with awesome patience, skill, humour and high expectation has urged me ever onward – and who graciously agreed to write the Foreword.

Last, but definitely not least, my family. My husband Graham, ever constant in his encouragement and with whom I share my life, and our children Claire and Daniel who are bearers and inspirers of infinite joy, laughter, love and hope. To them I dedicate this book.

SUSAN HARDWICK

ACKNOWLEDGEMENTS

The publishers wish to express their gratitude to the following for permission to include copyright material in this book:

Beacon Press, 25 Beacon Street, Boston, MA 02108, USA for extracts from *Man's Search for Meaning* by Viktor E. Frankl © 1959, 1962, 1984, 1992 by Viktor E. Frankl, Beacon Press, Boston.

Gujarat Sahitya Prakash, Anand, Gujarat, 388 001 India for extracts from *The Song of the Bird* by Anthony de Mello SJ.

David Higham Associates Ltd, 5-8 Lower John Street, Golden Square, London W1R 4HA for extracts from *Dante: The Divine Comedy*, trans. D. L. Sayers, published by Penguin.

Indiana University Press, 601 North Morton Street, Bloomington, IN 47404-3797, USA for the extract from *To Mend the World* by Emil Faekenheim.

Macmillan Publishers, 25 Eccleston Place, London SW1W 9NF for *The Coming* by R. S. Thomas taken from *Later Poems 1972-1982*, and the extract from *The Musician* by R. S. Thomas, taken from *Selected Poems 1946-1968*, published by Papermac and Macmillan General Books respectively.

Richard Scott Simon, 43 Doughty Street, London WC1N 2LF for the extract from *Night* by Elie Wiesel, published by Penguin.

Stainer & Bell Ltd, PO Box 110, Victoria House, 23 Gruneisen Road, Finchley, London N3 1DZ for the hymn text *For the healing of the nations* by Fred Kaan © Copyright 1968 Stainer & Bell Ltd.

© Control: the extract from *The Shade of His Hand* by Michael Walker.

Scripture quotations are taken from the *New Jerusalem Bible,* published by Darton Longman & Todd.

Every effort has been made to trace the owners of copyright material and we hope that no copyright has been infringed. Pardon is sought and apology is made if the contrary be the case and a correction will be made in any reprint of this book.

CONTENTS

AUSCHWITZ

AUSCHWITZ

Elimelekh of Lizensk, and his brother Zusia, journeyed for years in the 18th century seeking enlightenment and wisdom.

One tradition has it that every place they stayed – even if only for one night – became annexed to the Hasidic Kingdom; and that the places they could not reach remained outside Hasidim.

There is a curious legend that tells of the two brothers arriving in a small village near Cracow with the intention of staying overnight. But they were restless and felt compelled to leave.

As dusk fell, they left.

The name of the village: Auschwitz. (1)

Few people spoke on that three-hour journey to the death camp.

We walked into the camp, through the gates over which the slogan declaimed:

'Work is Freedom'

No words can describe the heavy and oppressive air that still hangs over the place. The very walls of the buildings seem to cry out with the pain and despair they have witnessed. How much more appropriate would have been the 'dead title' of Dante's inscription over Hell Gate:

Through me is the way to the City of Desolation.
Through me is the way to eternal suffering . . .
Abandon all hope, you who enter. (2)

The burden of history presses down heavier and heavier as horror succeeds horror.

The immense display cases each stretching twenty feet or more; filled with human hair, or tooth and shaving and hair brushes, or shoes, or spectacles, or suitcases bearing the names of their owners.

The special little showcase that contained the shoes, socks, dress, and bonnet of a ten-month-old child was almost unbearable. I thought of my own children when they were babies of that age, so full of potential as had been this little one; of how strong and intelligent and beautiful they are now, with so much realised and so much more to come – unlike this child whose potential had not had the opportunity to be realised before she had been injected into the heart with a life destroying substance.

On, into the punishment cells, the tortures inflicted thought up with a fiendish ingenuity. And on, further, through other nightmare scenarios until, eventually, we were standing before the gas chambers where women, children and old men together were ordered to strip naked before being marshalled into the 'showers'. In twenty minutes six hundred human beings, squeezed together in the long hangar-like room, could be gassed to death. Looking up at the ceiling you could still see the vents through which the deadly emissions poured.

Then the trucks onto which the bodies were piled for the short journey down the tracks to the great cylindrical ovens.

I wished I could weep, but it all went far too deep for the relief of tears. There was just this terrible sick ache in my heart and stomach, and a great, ever-increasing burden of sadness which bowed my shoulders with the weight of a cross, and grew ever heavier as scene succeeded scene.

Then on to Birkenau, Auschwitz's sister camp a few miles down the road, to where the trains packed with resistance fighters, homosexuals, gypsies and then, later, Jews used to come.

I stood on the spot where Dr. Josef Mengele had stood and silently pointed to the left, or to the right, according to whether each person lived or died.

'Mengele's task was to separate those to be murdered at once from those to be made to work now and murdered at a later date. Mengele was fond of performing his task on Yom Kippur: the time when [according to the Jewish faith] God judges who will live and who will die. To cite his own boast, it would be Mengele, and not God, that would judge what Jews would live and who to die.' (3)

A vivid picture came into my mind of Judgement Day, and of Mengele standing before God – who pointed silently downward. And what if he had repented before he had died – could God have forgiven even this, I wondered, as I listened to our guide tell of how a line had been strung a certain number of feet from the ground. All the children whose heads passed clear under the line were sent to the gas chambers: they were too small to be of any use as workers. Soon the children, in the uncanny and clear-sighted way they have, realised the line's significance; the little ones making pathetic and desperate attempts to walk tall enough in order that they might live.

Huts stretched as far as the eye could see. To the left for the women and children; to the right for the men.

Hundreds of prisoners packed each hut. Tiers of wooden-slatted bunks, each measuring about five feet by eight feet, and each sleeping seven or eight people, line the walls. I placed my hand on one of the bunks, carved with the identities of those who had lain there, and felt their presence engrained in the air as well as under my touch, just as their names were engraved in the wood.

Down the centre of the hut runs a stone slab. On this women gave birth, people were ill, and died.

Anna, whose father had been an inmate of Auschwitz for several years, has been acting as guide for many years now, but it is obvious that still she, too, suffers in the telling of the existence and the suffering of the inmates.

A wide, bare, strip of land separates the women's huts from those of the men.

At the far end is a great stone urn in which a flame burns constantly in memory of all that happened in these places, and

'LEST WE FORGET.'

Elie Wiesel, in his book *Night*, describes the dark horror of childhood years spent in those camps. The child who entered Auschwitz, aged twelve years, wanting to be a Rabbi when he grew up, left Birkenau, aged fifteen years, an atheist.

> The human spirit, outraged and humiliated beyond all that heart and spirit can conceive of, defied a divinity who was blind and deaf.
> That day I had ceased to plead. I was no longer capable of lamentation. On the contrary, I felt very strong. I was the accuser and God the accused. My eyes were open and I was alone – terribly alone in a world without God and without man. Without love or mercy. I had ceased to be anything but ashes, yet I felt myself to be stronger than the Almighty to whom my life had been tied for so long . . . From then on, life was to be one long night. (4)

Auschwitz

encompassing
and
representing
all the
pain
sorrow
and
cruelty
in the
world

and in
each
of
us

A Prayer for Good Friday

Christ our victim,
whose beauty was disfigured
and whole body torn upon the Cross;
open wide your arms
to embrace our tortured world,
that we may not turn away our eyes,
but abandon ourselves to your mercy.
Amen. (5)

BROKEN

This is me, broken for you.
(The teaching of Jesus of Nazareth)

On the noticeboard above my desk are two pictures.

One is of a little two-year-old Rwandan boy, crouched in a gutter, resting his forehead against the pavement edge in utter anguish. Deep despair, of the sort no small child should know, is etched into every line of that vulnerable body.

The second picture is of an old Bosnian couple. She is in an ancient wheelchair, clutching her handbag and a blanket in her lap, her feet held awkwardly to one side as there is no footrest. He is pushing the chair, and has another blanket draped around his shoulders. They have been unceremoniously and roughly turned out of their home by enemy soldiers, and are wearily struggling across rough ground that surely will soon shake the chair into pieces, into an unknown and fearful future. In the despair on their faces can be read, 'Is this the last journey we will make together in this life?'

Three broken, unidentifiable people plucked from the framework of their normal everyday lives; anonymous because it is the context that gives fragments their identity.

Three people who represent the individuals, families, communities and worlds that are broken and fallen apart: examples of the tears, the despair, the costliness, the waste of precious people.

They are ikons for me: fragments in a fractured world, desperately seeking that which will draw it, and hold it, all together. Placed alongside them is the single mother I know, struggling in Inner City, England, to raise her four children on Income Support. 'I take each day as it comes,' she says. 'I daren't look further; there is no future so far as I'm concerned.'

It is said that the broken pieces of a hologram each contain the complete picture of the hologram. Just so, my ikons represent for me all the broken people of the world. They remind me, too, that fragments are part of the whole picture, which is incomplete without them.

However, whilst we manage to split our thinking into fragments, and not to allow one area to affect another, nor even to understand how the areas are all designed to interlink and interlock, the world will continue to be a place of chaos, destruction, brokenness and despair.

Between each fragment of our broken world is a space, a dark place, into which Christians are called to follow Christ who, after his death, descended even into the darkness of hell to reclaim lost souls; and who calls us now to descend with him into the living hells of injustice, pain and fear.

Light places don't need light, but dark places do. With the gaps filled, what was broken becomes whole.

Simon Peter was one of Jesus' first disciples, and one of the most lovable and easiest to relate to because he tried so hard to get it right, but so often got it wrong.

He also overestimated himself at times; as when he emphatically declared to Jesus, 'Lord, I would be ready to go to prison with you, and to death.' To which Jesus replied, 'I tell you, Peter, by the time the cock crows today, you will have denied three times that you know me.'

They seized Jesus then and led him away, and took him to the high priest's house. Peter followed at a distance. They had lit a fire in the middle of the courtyard and Peter sat down among them, and as he was sitting there by the blaze, a servant-girl saw him, peered at him, and said, 'This man was with him too.' But he denied it. 'Woman, I do not know him,' he said. Shortly afterwards someone else saw

him and said, 'You are one of them too.' But Peter replied, 'I am not, my friend.' About an hour later another man insisted, saying, 'This fellow was certainly with him. Why, he is a Galilean.' Peter said, 'My friend, I do not know what you are talking about.' At that instant, while he was still speaking, the cock crowed, and the Lord turned and looked straight at Peter, and Peter remembered the Lord's words when he had said to him, 'Before the cock crows today you will have disowned me three times.' And he went outside and wept bitterly.
(Luke 22:54-62)

Peter has come face to face with the reality of himself.

For now he is a man broken by self-revelation and remorse – but, with the subsequent knowledge and reassurance of Jesus' forgiveness, he will recover and go on to achieve great things.

Of the churches dedicated to Peter in and around Jerusalem, the most poignant is the Church of St. Peter in Gallicantu, on the eastern slopes of Mount Zion. 'In Gallicantu' means 'at the crowing of the cock', and the church marks the spot where Peter is believed to have denied knowing Jesus.

An ancient stepped path leads from here to the Pool of Siloam where Jesus sent the man born blind, after he had put paste of spittle and mud on his eyes, to go and wash. After doing as Jesus told him, the man had come back able to see. (John 9) Jesus, it is said, used this path on his way from the Last Supper to the Garden of Gethsemane, just a short time after predicting Peter's denial and only hours before Peter fulfilled the prediction.

Broken on a Cross
for a world that seems
careless of your gift.
The fragments of your life
lie scattered
over the land
where you walked and
taught and
preached and
healed;
where you laughed and
wept and
played and
prayed:
like a shattered hologram
each piece reflecting
the complete picture.

REJECTION

God chose those who by human standards are common and contemptible indeed those who count for nothing – to reduce to nothing all those who do count for something.
(1 Corinthians 1:28)

It was a stiflingly hot August day in New York and I was hurrying to get to church on time. At the bottom of the great sweep of the cathedral steps sat a stick of a man, dressed only in shorts. He stared sightlessly at the passers-by who, in their turn, ignored him. On his lap he held a sign: 'Homeless and hungry'. Thinking I could give him some money after the service, I ran past him and up the steps as the clock intoned the hour and the priest the beginning of the service.

When I came out, nourished by the bread and wine of Communion, he had gone.

It was another very hot day and I had gone for a walk in the countryside near my home in England. Along a quiet road, coming towards me, was what appeared to be a mobile rag-bag. As it drew closer it turned into a girl of about seventeen years of age dressed in layer upon layer of coat and jersey and shirt strips, now scarcely recognisable as such, bound carefully around her body like winding sheets. Presumably-once-beautiful blonde hair, but now matted and dirty, framed a face set in an expression of acute misery.

As I stopped to speak to her she turned a warning look of such fierce pride towards me that the words of concern and help died unspoken on my lips. My outstretched hand was brushed aside. It seemed as if, stripped of innocence and reclothed in the knowledge of an uncaring world's rejection, she hugged to herself the only bit of power and choice she had left and she, in her turn, rejected me.

With no money in my pocket to give, no coat nor cardigan to urge upon her – I was dressed only in T-shirt and jeans – I watched as she walked away from me, aware of the sad, sad irony of it all: in New York I'd had the money but not the time. Now I had the time but nothing to give that was acceptable to this young girl.

Her pathetic figure was a blot against the clear beauty of God's creation; an indictment of humankind.

Of such situations was the story of the Good Samaritan born – told by Jesus two thousand years ago.

Will we ever get it right?

Returning to Jerusalem from visiting the Church of the Nativity in Bethlehem, which marks the spot where it is thought Mary gave birth to Jesus, we were stopped a couple of miles out of town at the checkpoint.

I was one of only two non-Palestinian passengers on the Arab bus. Just ahead of us in the queue was a taxi, at the rear window of which stood a soldier talking to the occupant. In his hand he held some pass papers. It is 1995, and Palestinians still have to carry passes in Israel; it is one of the parts of the Oslo Peace Agreement of two years ago which have not yet been implemented. After a few moments he handed the papers back through the window, and a young Palestinian woman in traditional dress climbed out of the taxi which was then waved on. In her arms she held a small baby. It was noon and very hot, and she had no other choice but to walk back to Bethlehem in the heat.

The soldiers, automatic rifles at the ready, climbed onto our bus, and I remembered another, similar checkpoint some years ago when I was crossing from East to West Berlin. There was the same halting in any conversation, the same tense stillness, each person staring straight ahead with unseeing eyes as each tried not to draw attention to himself or herself.

As I watched the young woman begin her journey back to Bethlehem I thought of the church I had just visited – and the mother and the baby boy it commemorated. She had had to give birth in a stable to the Saviour of the world because she, too, had been turned away.

The beautiful Dominus Flevit Church on the Mount of Olives is shaped like a teardrop.

It marks the place where, it is said, Jesus beheld Jerusalem before he entered the city for the last time, on Palm Sunday, and wept over it.

> As he drew near and came in sight of the city, he shed tears over it and said, 'If you too had only recognised on this day the way to peace! But in fact it is hidden from your eyes.' (Luke 19:41/42)

A stone pillar in the grounds of Dominus Flevit (the words mean 'The Lord's Tears') bears the following inscription:

> Here rings anew the love of God's lament:
> Mankind, made for himself,
> so far from him has strayed;
> here, now, the Saviour calleth thee in love;
> God calleth, calleth, calleth:
> 'Repent and come back home.'

Is it nothing to you, all you who pass by?

(Notice set against the great cross placed each Eastertide in
the marketsquare of an English Midlands town.)

High on a hill
standing in the shadow
beneath the bower of bare branches
of an ancient gnarled tree,
I looked through the
arthritic-curled limbs and fingers
stiff with age
and crowned with thorns,
at a world so achingly
bright and beautiful
and shot through
with the Son.
Berries of blood.
Shreds of sheep's fleece
hung and clung
in fronds
where they had brushed and touched
the spikes –
and then moved on.

INDIFFERENCE

All that is needed for evil to triumph is that good people do nothing.
(Reinhold Neibuhr)

When we hear, see, or read descriptions of the evils of Auschwitz and the other death camps, we shudder with horror and wonder how it could have happened. But there are 'little Auschwitzes' happening round us still all the time, powered by cruelty and violence and injustice and greed, and the outworking of fear or hate – or indifference.

On the outskirts of Jerusalem is the Mount of Olives, location of much of the drama of Jesus' ministry and, particularly, of his last days. Here, in the Garden of Gethsemane, on the night before fear and hate put him to death, Jesus spent time in anguished prayer.

Today the Church of All Nations stands close by, its name a symbol of man's recognition of God's longing for the oneness of humankind.

The service of Holy Communion was nearing completion. Those of us taking part were gathered round the sanctuary and had received the bread and the wine. The priest was about to give the final blessing.

At this still point, when all was quiet, suddenly, literally, it was as if hell had broken loose. With a whooshing roar, the chapel at one side of the main altar burst into flames which engulfed the entire area from floor to ceiling. Tongues of flame ran across the sanctuary carpet towards the priest.

For a moment or two everyone was transfixed where they knelt or stood. Then a guide ran, shouting, from the back of the church, breaking the spell, and fire extinguishers were hunted and found. It took some time to damp down the blaze but, throughout, there was no panic; more a sense of disbelief as to the reality of this seemingly apocalyptic event.

However, it transpired it was not, after all, a religious manifestation of either celestial or demonic origin, but a Molotov Cocktail.

I wonder – what events could have shaped the hate which motivated, and then drove, the young man who threw the bomb; and with such indifference as to whether innocent people were hurt or killed?

The word 'hate' is used so often and so carelessly in so many different situations that, like its opposite 'love', it has lost its ability to stop us in our tracks. Both 'love' and 'hate' are words which have become debased currency. But they are power-packed words, each containing a world of meaning, capable of expressing, as almost no other words can, our interior state.

Psychologists tell us that the two emotions are very near to one another, although I suspect those caught up in the consequences of either would take issue with that claim.

What was the emotion at the very heart of the cause of the Holocaust – a Greek word whose rough translation is 'destruction by fire' – the flames of which were so skilfully fanned into the furnaces that consumed millions of people?

One thing is certain: what happened then was the sum total of millions of individual contributions. All sorts and types of negative feelings, nurtured by all sorts and types of situations, within each person which were projected outwards on to a particular focus.

Lying dormant within most of us is a whole grey area which is neither love nor hate nor any other emotion, and which could most accurately be described as indifference. Indifference is no-feeling.

Indifference, as history has repeatedly shown, is far more deadly than hate, as it has been responsible for far more suffering. Indifferent people are the silent majority who look – and then turn their eyes away. But it is the reluctance to stand up and to speak out against injustice and wrong which allows situations of hate to grow and to flourish.

'The weathercock mind, the vague tolerance that will neither approve nor condemn. The cautious cowardice . . .' (6)

Jesus reserved his greatest condemnation for those 'who did not'.

He said:

> 'I was hungry and you never gave me food,
> I was thirsty and you never gave me anything to drink,
> I was a stranger and you never made me welcome,
> lacking clothes and you never clothed me,
> sick and in prison and you never visited me.'

Then it will be their turn to ask:

> 'Lord, when did we see you hungry or thirsty,
> a stranger or lacking clothes,
> sick or in prison and did not come to your help?'

And he will answer:

> 'In truth I tell you,
> in so far as you neglected to do this
> to one of the least of these,
> you neglected to do it to me.'
> (Matthew 25:42-45)

Third-World-hands held out pleading to First-World debt
collectors:
'Your tied-loan interest is bleeding us dry.
Help us! Or as a nation we die.'

Hard-headed-money-men, fingers tightly fisted round
government-sponsored deals,
look
and shrug
and turn away.

Huddled-in-doorways, bright-eyed hope dulled with hunger
and loneliness and fear, the homeless youth
– society's forgotten ones –
reach out to passers-by who
look
and shrug
and walk away.

Upwardly-socially-mobiles, ambitious and detached, lock
car windows as they
drive down-town roadways of
high rise and tenement and slum.
Offended by such unseemly sights, they
look
and shrug
and drive away.

Clear-eyed-innocence, across the playground spotted the
bullied child bullied yet again.
Running, and placing herself between tormentors and
tormented, she stands her ground, defends –
then
gently wipes
all tears away.

And God will wipe all tears from their eyes . . .
there will be no more mourning
or sadness
or pain.
(Revelation 21:4)

When they reached the place called The Skull,
there they crucified him and the two criminals,
one on his right,
the other on his left.

Jesus said:

'Father, forgive them;
they do not know
what they are doing.'
(Luke 23:33, 34)

SUFFERING

God was there, crying with me. He was powerless to do anything about it. But he suffered with me.
(Rabbi Hugo Gryn, survivor of Auschwitz, who was fifteen years of age when freed from the death camp.)

Since Jesus himself has passed through the test of suffering, he is able to help those who are meeting their test now.
(Hebrews 2:14)

He was one of the bravest men I have ever known. He suffered a very great deal, much of it on behalf of others, but he never once complained, nor showed any self-pity.

As a young man, in his spare time he set up and ran a theatre company, giving all the profits to charities and associations for children who were disabled. He was an accomplished sportsman, the riskier the sport the better. He ran his own business, and travelled the world. He was an achiever, and everything he touched seemed to turn to gold.

Then the charmed time seemed to end, though not by his definition. He lost an eye in a sporting accident; the Second World War came and there was no longer any demand for the luxury leather products his company made; finally the news that his accident had triggered off a rare syndrome, and his legs would have to be amputated.

As the illness was so rare the doctors asked him if he would give permission for them to experiment on him, so that others would benefit from the knowledge gained: it would not save his legs but it might save others. He gave the permission, but the result of the delay in operating was that the amputations were much more radical and severe.

The experiments and the after-effects, both short and

31

long term, were agonising.

However, his courage and determination were great. Within months he was walking so competently with his crutches that people did not believe he had artificial legs.

He was never out of, often severe, pain for the rest of his life, but he never appeared resentful and would, instead, joke saying with grim humour that he was dying on the instalment system – and, more seriously, that he was, in fact, a most fortunate man as he had a wonderful wife and four beautiful children.

My father died suddenly, fifteen years after losing his second leg, when I was fifteen years old. During those years, he continued to work at a full-time job, to drive an ordinary car, and to live a normal life. His legacy to all who knew him, and especially his family: memories of extra-ordinary courage in the face of suffering.

How we cope with suffering defines what sort of person we are.

Suffering is universal, so the problem of suffering, whether it be physical, mental, emotional or spiritual, affects us all.

To have the ability to suffer must be one of the definitions of being alive. An ability to suffer is our curse, but also our salvation, for it can be an early warning system that all is not well.

When you are in the midst of suffering it can feel total and all-absorbing, and so very lonely, for no one else can bear it for you.

Suffering makes people cry out 'Why?'

It is good to protest against one's own suffering; but it is vital that we protest against the suffering of others, and to cry out 'No!' It is hard to be alongside someone who suffers. To try to share their pain, but to be unable to do anything to ease it. By our very presence, though, that is precisely what we do.

Christ also cried out 'Why?' And 'No!'; then set about changing things. The Gospels are accounts of his journeying through suffering, others' as well as his own, and how he worked tirelessly, and at great personal cost, to alleviate all types of suffering wherever he went.

We may not have his gifts of healing, nor his power, but we can watch, and pray with, and stay alongside those who suffer. We can work to improve those social conditions which cause or increase the suffering. We can speak out against injustice, repression, neglect and torture: all things that cause untold amounts of suffering.

Jesus knew all about suffering alone:

> Then Jesus came with the disciples to a plot of land called Gethsemane; and he said to them, 'Stay here while I go over there to pray.' He took Peter, and the two sons of Zebedee, with him. And he began to feel sadness and anguish.
>
> Then he said to them, 'My soul is sorrowful to the point of death. Wait here and stay awake with me.' And going on a little further, he fell on his face and prayed. 'My Father,' he said, 'if it is possible, let this cup pass me by. Nevertheless, let it be as you, not I, would have it.'
>
> He came back to the disciples and found them sleeping, and he said to Peter, 'So you had not the strength to stay awake with me for one hour? Stay awake, and pray that you may be spared the test. The spirit is willing but the flesh is weak.'
>
> Again, a second time, he went away and prayed: 'My Father,' he said, 'if this cup cannot pass me by, but I must drink it, your will be done!'
>
> And he came back again and found them sleeping their eyes were so heavy.
>
> Leaving them there he went away alone and prayed for the third time, repeating the same words . . .
> (Matthew 26:36-44)

Next to the most ancient of the ancient olive trees in the Garden of Gethsemane is a plaque upon which are the following words:

O My Father,
if be possible, let this cup pass from me.
Nevertheless, not my will but thine be done.
(Luke 22:42)

You, O Jesus in Gethsemane,
in deepest night and agony,
spoke these words of surrender
and trust to God the Father.
In gratitude and love I want to say with you
in my hours of fear and trouble:
'My Father,
I do not understand you, but I trust you.'

Did it hurt when they all ran away?
And did it hurt when they scourged you?
And did it hurt when you fell by the way?
Did it hurt when they stripped you?
Did it hurt when they nailed you to the Cross?
Did it hurt when they mocked you
and did it hurt to see your mother there?

O yes, it hurt.
O yes, it hurt, my friend.
I knew all pain,
from head to toe,
inside and out.

And therefore, when you ask this question,
think hard if you believe in me –
that I am God
and that I am man,
and that I lived
and suffered
and died,
because I loved.
And now I live anew.

And so it is my turn to ask a question:
Do you believe all this?
Do you? (7)

DARKNESS

They came to Bethsaida, and some people brought to Jesus a
blind man whom they begged him to touch.
(Mark 8:22)

I wonder whether, when God created night and day, he was
also creating a parable of darkness and light.

Did he know in advance how we would treat this world
and each other, and so was there the pain of childbirth
woven into the joy of creating?

Were his dreams broken even before they were shaped
and formed?

Was his own pain part of his plan?

If he is beyond time, then Jesus' cry from his darkest
moment on the cross must have echoed, back to those first
moments of creation and been part of it, and on into eternity.

> As the letter to the Ephesians says: God chose us
> in Christ before the world was made to be holy and
> faultless before him in love, marking us out for
> himself beforehand to be adopted daughters and
> sons, through Jesus Christ. (Ephesians 1:4, 5)

To know that your carefully conceived, your precious
plan, will bring such disappointment and bitter sorrow and
yet to go ahead with it implies a steadfastness and constancy,
a level of commitment, that takes one's breath away. He
must have so wanted us, and hoped against all the evidence
that we would not turn day back into night.

> I look up at your heavens, shaped by your fingers,
> at the moon and the stars you set firm –
> what are human beings that you spare a thought for me,
> or the child of Adam that you care for me?

Yet you have made me little less than a god,
you have crowned me with glory and beauty,
made me lord of the works of your hands,
put all things under my feet . . .
(Psalm 8:3-6 adapted)

And yet, knowing all of this, I still insist on walking too often in the dark side of the valley, stumbling over unseen obstacles, knowing emptiness, despair and disillusionment when the going gets too tough.

Over the other side the valley is radiant with light.

My erratic journeying takes me first to one side, then to the other. When in the sun too long, I'm drawn to the shade but, when there, I long to return to the caressing warmth of the Son.

There is a darkness about suffering which makes the pain, whether physical, mental or emotional, so much harder to bear. Another can come alongside in silent or vocal sympathy, but no one else can bear the pain for you. Sometimes, in our anguish and need, we can simultaneously accept and reject the proffered hand.

Most of us fear the darkness at some level in our being. It is a fear that reaches back into earliest childhood memories, experiences and fantasies.

The deepest and blackest despair to many, though, is the fear that God has abandoned them to their nightmare.

I was doing my rounds as hospital chaplain, and it was visiting time as I made my way down this particular ward. The buzz of chatter accentuated the silence of the visitor seated beside the bed of a young woman at the far end who appeared to be asleep.

I was drawn to them. My first word of greeting had scarcely been spoken when the young man, looking up and seeing who I was, leapt to his feet and seized my outstretched hand in a tight grip.

A torrent of words fell from his lips, getting louder and more forcible as moment succeeded moment, until he was shouting. Tears ran freely down his face.

The ward hushed until only his voice rang round the now silent room, but he was oblivious to everyone. I don't think he even saw me as me: I was merely a focus for his deep distress and despair. Through the torrent of words I began to understand that his young wife, who had made a number of suicide attempts over the previous couple of years, seemed to have succeeded this time and was slipping slowly towards death. She could live but had lost the will to do so; being put in a public ward rather than a side room was a last attempt to rouse her from her deep apathy.

'How could a loving God have allowed all this to happen?' he sobbed. 'If he does exist, if he cares, why doesn't he save her? He must be cruel and heartless . . . a fiend, a devil. Where is he? How could you worship, and represent, such a God? You must be a devil, too.'

The questions, the accusations, the terrible sorrow and anger, poured over me without a pause. At first I tried to answer then, seeing it was not helping, I was silent and just absorbed it as best I could, until tears ran down my face, too.

Yet, all this time, his tight grip on my hand never slackened.

Then suddenly he stopped as quickly as he had begun, and slumped back into his chair, lost somewhere far down within himself.

It was a long time before he let go of my hand. When he did his fingermarks were printed deep into my skin and had bruised it. Meanwhile, I sat beside him in silence, sensing that he did not want any more words – just someone to share the darkness with him.

From the sixth hour there was darkness over all the land until the ninth hour.

And about the ninth hour Jesus cried out in a loud voice, 'My God, my God, why have you forsaken me?' . . . Then Jesus, again crying out in a loud voice, yielded up his spirit.

And suddenly, the veil in the sanctuary was torn in two from top to bottom, the earth quaked, the rocks were split, the tombs opened . . .

The centurion, together with the others guarding Jesus, had seen the earthquake and all that was taking place, and they were terrified and said, 'In truth, this man was son of God.'
(Matthew 27:45, 46, 50-52, 54)

Sunlight stealing softly over
the sheep-littered
hills into the shadowed
valley where I sat.
Silence turned into gold
broken only by the scolding
of ducks on the pond.

Suddenly, slicing the
stillness in two, jets
like great black birds
screamed overhead and
toward the horizon
rolling up the golden light
in their slipstream and
leaving the valley
and the world in
deepest shadow.

EMMAUS

THE JOURNEY CONTINUES

It was an upstairs room, ready and prepared for the Passover Supper. The table was laid with the lamb and herbs, the wine and the bread.

The stage was set for the final act of the greatest drama since the creation of the universe.

It is difficult to imagine the importance of that night: what it must have been like to be there. It seems that the disciples had only a partial understanding of the eternal significance of those moments; their minds still encased in tombs of ignorance, with stones rolled across entrances.

Perhaps, though, it would have been impossible for it to have been any other way.

Could human minds, however enlightened, have possibly been able to embrace, all at once and in its entirety, its implications for all peoples for all times.

Was it, in fact, the gentle mercy of God that allowed understanding to dawn gradually, at a pace they could cope with, so that it literally would not blow their minds?

That gradual and progressive dawning of understanding, reaching into the dark recesses of hearts and minds, is one which resonates with our experience. Every so often there are flashes of insight coming through people or events or experiences of one sort or another which light up the way, and us, and which, hopefully, change us and move us on.

We are like the travellers on the Emmaus road who did not discern the implications of Jesus' crucifixion, who did not recognize Jesus when he came up and walked and talked with them and explained how it had to be so: that it was foreshadowed in the Scriptures that Christ should suffer before entering into his glory – and who finally recognised him in the breaking of the bread at Supper; but he had vanished from their sight.

Again, perhaps it had to be so. He could not be fully present to them in the bread if he was also present physically: the one took over from the other.

From now on they would never break bread without his presence being reincarnated for them.

Their eyes had been opened, and now they could see clearly.

They would still make mistakes; would still sin, repent, be forgiven, only to stumble yet again as they continued their journey along the Emmaus road towards Jerusalem. But now it would be different: they would be journeying in the company of the Risen Christ, unseen but constantly present through his Spirit.

On the night before he died, at that Last Supper, Jesus had said to his disciples:

I shall ask the Father and he will give you
another advocate
to be with you for ever,
the Spirit of truth whom the world can never accept
since it neither sees nor knows him;
but you know him,
because he is with you, he is in you.

I shall not leave you as orphans;
I shall come to you.
In a short time the world will no longer see me;
but you will see that I live
and you also will live.

On that day
you will know that I am in my Father
and you in me
and I in you . . .

The Holy Spirit,
whom the Father will send in my name,
will teach you everything
and remind you of all that I have said to you.
(John 14:16-20, 26)

And so I turn from Auschwitz,
though it will stay in my mind always,
and set my face toward Jerusalem.

I turn from the City of Hell;
in which many heavenly acts were lived out of pure
bravery,
generosity,
unselfishness,
and gifting of self
to others and for others.

Our purpose in living
is to bring meaning into the lives of others.
Suffer we may,
but we must do it willingly, meaningfully,
for others may be dependent upon us doing so. (8)

(Viktor Frank, Jewish psychologist, survivor of Auschwitz
and Birkenau, who brought meaning and purpose into many
lives in those places, thus helping many others to survive.)

This is me,
broken for you.
Now it is your life
that is bread
to be broken and shared,
so others may live.
(The teaching of Jesus Christ)

Extra-Ordinarily Ordinary

It was my first celebration of the Eucharist
as a newly-ordained priest,
eight months into my journey from Auschwitz,
and thirteen months before Jerusalem:
a wonderful, a perfect day.

Earlier that same day had been the Ordination Service,
two and a half hours in length but, during which, time
seemed suspended
so marvellous was the music, the choreography,
the ceremonial and colour.
And all set within the rich symbolism
of Coventry Cathedral.

It was an evening celebration of Holy Communion.

As I said the words of consecration over
the bread and the wine
for the first time, I felt that all my past,
my present, and my future
were drawn together and connected at this point.
And not only my own past, present and future but the
past, present and future
of the universe as well.

I was in a long, long line of countless numbers of people,
stretching back and linking to that first supper,
who had celebrated this holiest of mysteries,
and would celebrate it into the future.

At this eternal moment we, and all who had ever
received the bread of life and the cup of salvation in faith,
became one,

as we do each time we break bread
in Christ's name;
for it is then that we are all drawn together in his saving act
upon the Cross.

It all felt so right; so ordinary.

Extra-ordinarily ordinary.

A Journeying Prayer

SOUL OF CHRIST

Jesus,
may all that is you
flow into me.
May your body and blood
be my food and drink.
May your passion and death
be my strength and life.
Jesus,
with you by my side,
enough has been given.
May the shelter I seek
be the shadow of your Cross.
Let me not run
from the love
that you offer,
but hold me safe
from the forces
of evil.
On each of my dyings
shed your light
and your love.
Keep calling to me
until that day comes,
when, with all your saints,
I may praise you for ever.

Amen. (9)

Gathering Up The Fragments

Jesus said to his disciples, 'Pick up the pieces left over, so that nothing is wasted.'
(John 6:12 – The feeding of the five thousand)

In this story could it be that the fragments were the focus of the story, the central figures, rather than the main crowd?

It would be typical of Jesus to pay more attention to those on the edge, the forgotten ones, the powerless ones, the unimportant and the put-aside; to seek them out and to gather them in, for: 'the will of the One who sent me is that I should lose nothing of all that he has given me.' (John 6:39)

And so the fragments of our broken world are lovingly, tenderly, drawn together, gathered up and healed.

Whilst on holiday in Wales once, one evening we watched a shepherd and his dog rounding up sheep from a craggy, heather-clad mountainside.

Most of the sheep responded to the worrying of the dog who, in her turn, responded to the beautiful and intricate whistled commands of her master. But there was one young sheep who, in its fear and bewilderment, scrambled further and further up and away, until it was penned in by some rocks over a precipice.

At much risk to himself, the shepherd climbed up and patiently, gently, calmed it before guiding it back down the hillside to join the rest of the flock.

One of the most profound things that the Gospels tell us is Jesus' commitment to, and care of, individuals. Every single person mattered, whoever they were, however unimportant and lowly, or undeserving.

You get the sense that he would have gladly gone anywhere, would have suffered anything and even died, if just to save one person; to Jesus, each person was the world, and contained the world of meaning.

In Dante's *Divine Comedy*, Virgil tells Dante how the rocks were dislodged by the earthquake which took place at the hour of Christ's descent into hell after his Crucifixion to look for, and to claim, lost souls:

> On the day
> When that great Prince to the First Circle above
> Entered, and seized from Dis the mighty prey
> Shortly ere He came, the deep foul gulf did move
> On all sides down to the centre, till I thought
> The universe trembled in the throes of love . . . (10)

Schindler was a German Nazi during the Second World War who, at great risk to himself, saved many hundreds of Jews from the gas chambers.

In gratitude, some of the survivors gave him a ring made from the gold fillings they had taken from their teeth.

On the ring was engraved, 'To save one person is to save a universe.'

In the Old City of Jerusalem there is a central point at which the four Quarters – Armenian, Christian, Muslim and Jewish – converge. Here, at the place of potential, a soldier is always on duty.

In one of the Quarters, I met with a Palestinian Christian who is leader of the music group, Al Baraem. The group write their own lyrics, about the things they yearn for and dream about; not just for themselves but for everyone. Songs about peace, human dignity, justice and equality, and love.

In 1993 they, and a Jewish music group, were chosen to play and to sing in Oslo at the signing of the Peace Agreement by Yassar Arafat and Yitzak Rabin. Jews and Arabs, coming together as one, making music and making peace together.

However, Oslo will be a shop-window display, of benefit only to the wider world of onlookers, until there is justice and until Arabs and Jews are making real and genuine peace within the Land of Israel itself.

At that point, the lyrics of Al Baraem will not be dreams but reality.

On the night that the Cathedral Church of Coventry burned, just one victim of the heavy bombing raid that destroyed so much of the city, two great roof timbers fell to the floor, one slanted over the other in a shape reminiscent of the Cross of Christ.

Provost Howard wrote soon after:

All night long
the city burnt, and her Cathedral burnt with her –
emblem of the eternal truth that when people suffer
God suffers with them.
Yet the tower still stood
with its spire soaring to the sky –
emblem of God's over-ruling majesty and love
which will help us to survive the suffering
and build a city and world founded on eternal love.

The great Charred Cross, formed from the two timbers, is a
central part of the new Cathedral's understanding of itself, and
its ministry in and to a suffering world.

Lord,
you searched
and found all
the fragments of me
scattered over the
path of my life.
Sharp bits, scuffed bits
and pieces worn smooth
with the wearing of the years.
Each broken shard
lovingly, tenderly held
drawn together
gathered up
shaped
and fitted into place.

Then –
the firing:
a painful part. Yet
in the furnace still
your hands cup me
and hold me
firm and constant in
their grasp.
The Love that will
not let me go
burning brighter and
hotter
than the flames
to cleanse and heal and seal.

Now –
at last
the pot stands
ready to be filled
with good things;
stronger for having been
broken
and re-formed
and re-created.

FORGIVING

*When wounds heal, scars are formed. But God sees them, not
as blemishes, but as marks of his glory.*
(Mother Julian of Norwich)

Rising out of the rubble and destruction of the Second
World War like the legendary Phoenix from its ashes, the
new Coventry Cathedral stands beside the bombed ruins of
the old.

The old building and the new are united by a covered
walkway, and neither would be complete without the other.
The ruins are not a blemish, but a mark of the glory of
reconciliation wrought by God's grace.

Both bear witness to the costliness of alienation, and of
the subsequent absolute requirement for forgiveness and
reconciliation: not only in times of international conflict, but
in the ordinary, the everyday, situations of life.

Some years ago, I had the misfortune to work for someone
who made my worklife very difficult indeed, and badly
dented my self-confidence. He had never worked closely
with a woman before, and obviously found the whole
situation very threatening.

It was a long time before I was able to leave. When I
finally moved on, my anger and hurt and dislike of him
lingered although I tried to let them go. The words of the
Lord's Prayer – 'Forgive us our sins as we forgive those who
sin against us' – challenged me, but did not change things. It
is difficult to forgive someone for wrongs done to you when
they appear neither to feel remorse, nor even to recognise
the damage and pain they have caused.

However, 'time is a great healer' is an old saw, but very

true. Gradually, I began to perceive that the person who was affected by my lack of forgiveness was not him, but me.

Then, one day, the work of grace was complete, and I knew I had forgiven him, not only with my head, but with my heart, too. I had not forgotten the injustices and hurts, but the wounds had healed, and the scars formed.

It was only then that I understood how imprisoned I had been by my lack of forgiveness. I suppose that, in letting go of my anger and the painful memories, and in reaching out in forgiveness, even though he was unaware of it, I had set him free – but the real freedom was mine. The negative feelings that had been eating away at me, bit by bit, were gone. Now I could move on into the future without that particular burden holding me back.

Jesus, though, in the way that he has, challenges us with something even more radical in what he says to Peter after Peter's profession of faith:

> . . . whatever you bind on earth
> will be bound in heaven;
> whatever you loose on earth
> will be loosed in heaven.
> (Matthew 16:19b)

Our lack of forgiveness has huge consequences for those against whom we bear a grudge.

The bustling, modern and charmless town of Tiberias stands as sharp contrast beside the still and ancient waters of the Sea of Galilee: Jesus' sea.

It was on one of the many occasions that I spent at the water's edge, caught and held by its beauty and thinking of the events it had witnessed, that I met Zak and 'Tiger' and heard their story.

The English translation of Tiger's Muslim name belied the gentleness of nature that was quickly apparent. Some years ago, his was one of the many Palestinian villages that had been razed to the ground by Israeli soldiers. In a few hours all that had marked generations of his family's presence in that place had been erased. The vineyards that had provided the means of livelihood, the house, the garden, all that had framed his life until then. Over this destruction, trees had been planted, as was the custom. But the prickly pear, common sight in such villages, is not so easily eradicated and has grown through amongst the trees, as symbol and reminder of all that once was.

Zak had been a soldier; though not part of what had happened to Tiger's village. Tragedy had hit his life with equal force when a Hamas bomb had killed, along with a number of other people, his wife and child.

Chance had brought these two men together, and common grief and suffering had bonded rather than separated them. They had decided to make a choice for friendship, as a demonstration of the triumph of the forces of light over the forces of darkness, of peace over conflict. It had not been easy, for many chose to misunderstand, and they had become alienated from former friends, and from members of their families. But there was a serenity about both men, and a strength as they seek to live out the wisdom they have learned through most bitter experience, that the forgiveness and healing between nations begins at the individual level.

The water lapping at our feet was a symbol of God's forgiveness in Jesus.

The sunlight casting our shadows upon the sea was reminder of the short span of our human lives against the backdrop of eternity.

In that brief moment which is our earthly existence we cannot afford to delay forgiveness.

The words of the following prayer, found in the clothing of an anonymous dead child in Ravensbruck Concentration Camp, challenge our smallness of mind and lack of forgiveness with their immensity of heart and spirit.

O Lord, remember not only the men
and women of good will,
but also those of ill will.

But do not remember all the suffering
they have inflicted upon us:

instead remember the fruits we have borne
because of the suffering –

our fellowship, our loyalty to one another, our humility, our
courage, our generosity,

the greatness of heart that has grown from this trouble.

When our persecutors come to be judged by you, let all of
these fruits that we have borne be their forgiveness. (11)

I made my sin known to you,
did not conceal my guilt.
I said, 'I shall confess
my offence to God.'
And you, for your part, took away my guilt,
forgave my sin.
(Psalm 32:5)

No need to remember past events,
no need to think about what was done before.
Look! I am doing something new.
Now it emerges, can you not see it?
I am making a road in the desert
and rivers in wastelands . . .
for my people, my chosen one to drink.
(Isaiah 43:18-20)

RECONCILING

All have sinned and fallen short of the glory of God.
(The opening words of the Litany of Reconciliation of
Coventry Cathedral, used each week at an open air
celebration of the Communion in the ruins at the altar upon
which is a charred cross and, behind which, are the words
'Father forgive . . .')

For many years, the two cities of Dresden and Coventry
have been united in their common wartime experience of
very heavy bombing. Since then the work of forgiveness and
reconciliation has been acted out in many ways between
these two communities.

On the fiftieth anniversary of the bombing of the city of
Dresden there was a commemoration concert in Coventry
Cathedral.

The musicians played against the backdrop of the great
glass wall upon which are etched angels and archangels
playing their own, heavenly, music. Beyond, the ruins – the
'old self' of the Cathedral – glowed golden under the night
lights of the city; a reminder of the cost of conflict, not only
within the world but within each individual, which is where
all conflict begins.

The visual drew you out to the ruins, symbol of the
aspiration and the destruction of humankind and of each
human being. The sound of the music drew you back into
the rebuilt Cathedral, symbol of forgiveness, of healing, and
of hope.

By day, it is the east-facing baptistry window – at right-
angles to the great glass screen which is now colourless –
that glows with light, for Coventry Cathedral is, unusually,

built on a north/south rather than an east/west axis.

In the morning, biblically traditionally a time of God's favour, any sunlight is picked up and magnified into a rainbow kaleidoscope, which pours its liquid colours over the font and across the floor to the steps of the Chapel of Unity on the far side.

'Do you turn to Christ?' 'Do you repent of your sins?' 'Do you renounce evil?' these questions are asked of those about to be baptised, or of the parents and godparents of the children too small to speak for themselves. It is a moment of solemn decision, of commitment, of repentance and forgiveness, of the laying down of a former way of living and the taking up of a new life in Christ.

Guilt can paralyse one into a frozen state of being, but integral to forgiveness is the requirement to change, to stand up and to walk purposefully into a new way of living and of being. If we want to change the world, we must first change ourselves, and then live out that change.

Reconciliation is the next step along the Emmaus road from forgiveness, and requires the admission of any responsibility for the situation by both sides. Forgiveness reaches down within oneself and so can be a solitary activity, but reconciliation requires a reaching out and a touching between the injured and the perpetrator.

> If you are bringing your offering to the altar
> and there remember that your brother or sister
> has something against you,
> leave your offering there before the altar,
> go and be reconciled with your brother first,
> and then come back and present your offering.
> (Matthew 5:23, 24)

All have sinned and fallen short of the glory of God.
The hatred which divided nation from nation,
race from race, class from class.
The covetous desires of people and nations
to possess what is not their own.
The greed which exploits the work of human hands
and lays waste the earth.
Our envy of the welfare and happiness of others.
Our indifference to the plight of the imprisoned,
the homeless, the refugee.
The lust which dishonours the bodies of men,
women and children.
The pride which leads us to trust in ourselves
and not in God.

Father forgive.

Be kind to one another, tenderhearted,
forgiving one another, as God in Christ forgave you.

God was in Christ reconciling the world to himself.
He has entrusted us with the message of reconciliation.
When anyone is united to Christ there is a new world;
the old order is gone; a new order is already begun.
In Christ's name be reconciled to God.

(From *The Litany of Reconciliation Service of Coventry Cathedral*)

Never to break anything which carries life itself; to
love, because to love is to live, and to give life.
(The credo of Father Bruno Hussar)

Set on a hill between the modern city of Tel Aviv and the
ancient city of Jerusalem is the village of Neve Shalom.

It is the realisation of a dream of reconciliation by Father
Bruno Hussar, born a Jew, who became a Christian, but
who values and treasures his Jewish roots.

'Everything in this land begins with a dream,' Father Bruno
told me.

His dream was of a community where Palestinians and
Jews would live and work together, the children growing
and learning and playing side by side, and one with another:
people committed to living together and ready to pay the
price of such unity.

The residential community of Neve Shalom numbers
ninety people: forty-five Jews and forty-five Palestinians, and
fifty of these are children. Together they live out the dream of
reconciliation in their daily lives. Children from neighbouring
villages come here to school, where the emphasis is on one's
own identity but also respect for, and openness to, the other
and a desire to know as much as one can about the other.

Many peace activities radiate from Neve Shalom around
Israel and into the wider world. There is a School of Peace
where Palestinians and Jews can come for a few days with
the motivation of learning to listen to the other – not as you
would like them to be, but as they are.

The concentration is upon young people, because they are
more clear-sighted and flexible, and over fifteen thousand
have passed through seminars here in the twenty-five years
since it all began. Further opportunities to carry on meeting
are provided throughout Israel. It is interesting that parents
often object to their children being involved in all of this.

Many thousand more, adults and young people, come for open days, and to visit informally.

'We have been given ten international Peace prizes,' Father Bruno said, 'and nominated five times for the Nobel Peace Prize. Each time I have prayed it will not be, and been glad when we have not received it, for it could be like wine going to the head. We are still too young.'

The stories of the difficulties overcome, and the early privations endured by Father Bruno and his friends in order to realise their dream – 'But we were young then,' he says, now eighty-four years of age and so a mere sixty then – would cover many pages.

It is a story of determination, courage, steadfastness and perserverance but, above all, a listening to God. And then faithfully responding to his will, however costly this might turn out to be.

'There is a mystical identification between people here and now, and Jesus,' said Father Bruno. 'Don't you think,' he asked, ' Jesus will say "I was hungry for reconciliation"?'

My people will live in a Neve Shalom (peaceful home)
in peaceful houses, tranquil dwellings . . .
(Isaiah 32:18)

True reconciliation is costly, a touching of hand and heart:
not enough for black to clasp white
but with drawn-down blind
on untransformed
heart and mind.
True reconciliation led Christ to the Cross
– and beyond.

True reconciliation is arms opened wide
– and a pierced side.

HEALING

*Jesus said, 'Which of these is easier: to say to the paralytic,
"Your sins are forgiven," or to say, "Get up, pick up your
stretcher and walk"? But to prove to you that the Son of man
has the authority to forgive sins on earth,' he said to the
paralytic, 'I order you, get up, pick up your stretcher, and go
off home.'*

*And the man got up, and at once picked up his stretcher
and walked out in front of everyone.*
(Mark 2:9-12)

As soon as you enter Coventry Cathedral, with the ruins of
the former building at your back, you are greeted by eyes
that catch you and hold you and follow you wherever you
go.

They are the eyes of the Risen Christ in Glory tapestry
that covers a complete wall, measuring almost seventy-five
feet by thirty-eight feet. This tapestry has caused much
controversy and argument ever since the new Cathedral was
consecrated: and that is really as it should be, for Jesus, in
his earthly life, was supremely controversial and so it is
fitting that the tapestry should reflect this aspect of him.

Whatever you may think of the rest of it, the head of
Christ must surely rate as one of the most spiritual works of
art.

I first saw it, and was captivated by it, twenty years ago.
And for twenty years a print, mounted on a block of wood,
has been an ikon for me: a precious means by which I am
drawn, as ikons do, through the image into mystery.

For me, Christ's expression becomes by turn sad, joyful,
wistful, warning, humorous, strong, vulnerable, and, always,
so real. But it is the eyes that, above all, challenge me and
draw me into their depths.

Each time I stand before that tapestry of woven grace and

glory and receive the bread and wine of the eucharist, his eyes meet mine, penetrating through to the core of my being with a gaze no longer of reproof, but of understanding, and love, and acceptance, and healing.

> I shall instruct you and teach you the way to go;
> I shall not take my eyes off you.
> (Psalm 32:8)

> Your eyes kiss mine,
> I see the love in them shine,
> I know that I'm in heaven right then;
> when your eyes kiss mine.
> (Folk Song)

As I made my way towards the Pilgrims' Gate which leads into the Old City of Jerusalem, scene of so many of Jesus' acts of healing, I saw a leper.

He was seated beside the road, pouring water first over his head, and then over the open, running sores and ulcers of his leprous leg.

It was noon, and the hot summer sun beat down upon him, for there was no shade.

After a while he struggled to his feet, and limped painfully on through the Gate.

At one end of the Via Dolorosa, the Way of the Cross, is St. Stephen's Gate at the opposite end of the Old City from the Pilgrim Gate.

Nearby, is the Pool of Bethesda, or Place of Mercy, where Jesus healed the man who had been ill for thirty-eight years. However, before he did anything, Jesus first asked him, 'Do you want to be well again?'

Jesus confronts all who experience weariness, fears, remorse, sickness of all kinds, with the same question. He asks us to leave our false values, to draw close to the Father, and so to enter a new wholeness and peace. To pass from death to life. (John 5:1f.)

On a wall, in the ruins of the Old Cathedral of Coventry, is a plaque upon which are the following words:

> Hallowed be thy name
> in Suffering –
> God be with me in my pain
> and in my enduring.

It is one of a number of plaques, forming a journey of prayer around the ruined walls.

Nearby, is the statue unveiled on 6th August 1995, in commemoration of the fiftieth anniversary of the bombing of Hiroshima and Nagasaki.

It is of two figures carved in bronze, each leaning toward the other over the space that lies between, and embracing. Their bodies form an arc, rising from and arching over the tomb-like brick base.

An identical statue was unveiled in Hiroshima three weeks previously. At each ceremony were representatives of the other country and community.

For the healing of the nations,
Lord, we pray with one accord;
for a just and equal sharing
of the things that earth affords.
To a life of love in action
help us rise and pledge our word.

Lead us, Father, into freedom,
from despair your world release;
that, redeemed from war and hatred,
all may come and go in peace.
Show us, how through care and goodness
fear will die and hope increase. (12)

Dawning

Jesus took the blind man by the hand. Then, putting spittle on his eyes and laying his hands on him, he asked, 'Can you see anything?'

The man, who was beginning to see, replied, 'I can see people; they look like trees as they walk around.'
(Mark 8:23, 24)

For several years, a major area of my work has been with people with disabilities.

This work has included being chaplain to a further education residential and day college for students with physical and sensory disabilities.

Part of these young people's life journey is coming to terms with, sometimes major, disabilities. This is particularly a challenge to those who have become disabled through accident or illness: one moment their life is full of one sort of dream and ambition – the next, these ambitions and dreams lie crumbled and broken. Before they can frame alternatives, they have to come to a new understanding of what is appropriate in their present situation.

This is true, too, of faith questions, whether their disability is congenital or acquired. Even those who would profess no particular beliefs often find that, at one point or another on their journey, they come face to face with fundamental questions.

'How could a loving God have allowed this to happen to me/made me like this?' is something I am often asked, in one form or another. Grappling with such huge questions produces a faith that is real: has to be real, if it is to nurture and to sustain.

For these fun-loving, life-affirming, often highly-gifted young people, physical and emotional pain, disappointment, frustration, rejection, prejudice, and the too-early death of friends, are part of their experience. But they also know how to wring out of life all that it has to offer, and they challenge and stretch themselves to achieve high-set goals, often overcoming huge odds in order to do so.

Not for them the well-manicured Jesus in spotless garments, worshipped by so many others; rather the dusty, travel-weary, foot-blistered, often reviled and rejected man-of-the-road.

Not for them the sanitised Christ on right angled cross, with coyly arranged loincloth to cover the embarrasing bits; rather the blind young man that I saw in Coventry Cathedral one day: searching, exploring and sensing arms and hands outstretched, body pressed close, to the great crown of thorns that forms the wall at the entrance to the Chapel of Gethsemane

On the wall-mosaic behind the altar, the Chalice of the Eucharist, which is also the Cup of Salvation, is held out to him.

High on the Mount of Beatitudes, a lovely small church is set amidst a profusion of exotic flowers, ferns and palms which blaze with colour in the clean, clear air.

Everything seems filled with, and surrounded by, light.

I found a quiet corner in the gardens, away from the many other people, where I could reflect upon the awesomely challenging words that Jesus had preached, from this very hillside, in the Sermon on the Mount. (Matthew 5:1-7:29; Luke 6:20-end)

Reading the familiar words in their original setting gave to them fresh power, and to me, deeper understanding.

I watched the crowds many of whom, as on that first occasion, had come looking for light. And I prayed that I, and they, would not lose the revelations received in this place when we left the mountain and returned to the plain.

Another mountain, and scene of another revelation of Jesus to his disciples. This time of his Transfiguration, near the small town of Nazareth. Again I tried to picture the scene and how the disciples must have felt as witnesses to such amazing and extraordinary events, and wondered how would I have reacted.

Peter exclaims how good it is to be there, and then, in his confusion and uncertainty, suggests building three shelters: one for Jesus, one for Moses and one for Elijah. Does he really think that Moses and Elijah are staying? Or is he desperately trying to delay the moment when he and John and James will have to leave the mountainside and return to the ordinariness of the plain?

Night gives way
to day as the
rose-coloured fingers of
dawning understanding
trail a path
across the morning
sky.

I look out from erstwhile
darkened sight
on a world
where
'Forests walk and
fishes fly
and figs grow
upon thorns':
a world turned
upside down
by a man who
spits on mud and
daubs my eyes.

I begin to see
there is method in
your madness;
you take the raw
materials of creation
and
mix them with your own
kneading them
blending them
until they are
one –

And that
is
what you do
with me.

JERUSALEM

JERUSALEM

Jerusalem, O Jerusalem,
rainbow city set
within a rainbow land.
What human artist's palette could paint
your myriad colours.
City of confusion, and of breathtaking beauty,
over whom Jesus shed such bitter tears.
Your beauty
his tears
intertwine
still today.

I rejoiced with those who said to me,
Let us go to the house of the Lord . . .
Our feet are standing
in your gates, O Jerusalem.
(Psalm 122:1, 2)

Jerusalem lies on the edge of the Judean Desert.

Each stone has its own history and legend and grace. And each
sunset in the clear air of the Judean hills seems to confirm the
ancient legend that, when God created the world, nine out of
ten measures of beauty were bestowed on the land of Israel,
and nine-tenths of Israel's beauty granted to Jerusalem.

Here, five thousand years ago, an early Bronze-age
settlement was established beside the waters of the Gihon
Spring, which grew and became a Canaanite city for the
next two thousand years.

Here King David, having captured it from the Jebusites in
about 1,000 BC, established Jerusalem as the capital of his

kingdom Israel, and here his son Solomon built the First Temple as the Sanctuary of the Ark of the Law and Covenant.

When Assyria besieged Jerusalem three hundred years later, the City's King Hezekiah had a tunnel bored through the rocks so that the waters of the Gihon Spring would flow inside the city into the Pool of Siloam. It was to this Pool that Jesus was to send a blind man to wash, whose eyes he had daubed with a paste of mud and his spittle, and who came back with sight fully restored.

Outside the gates of the Old City, Jesus was later crucified.

Jerusalem's history is conquest-ridden. Two thousand more turbulent years have passed since that most momentous of all moments in the history of the world, during which time Jerusalem has been ruled by either Christians, Jews or Muslims.

Today, the New City of Jerusalem is full of modern shops, hotels, and the bustling commercial life of any major conurbation. The roads are full of impatient drivers whose brake pedals seem to be attached to their car horns. Every time the traffic halts, even for a moment, a cacophony of horns assails the ears. It is as if there is a latent tension within each person which spills over in situations of frustration, such as traffic jams. A resident told me that during times when Israel has been in conflict with her neighbours, as in the Six-Day War, the horns stop: the tension is finding expression elsewhere.

The highly political, and highly charged atmosphere, of East Jerusalem is witness to many scenes of Palestinian-Israeli tension. And here one may experience life in an Arab country without the trouble of stepping outside Israel.

At the very heart of Jerusalem, pulsing with the sense of its ancient history, lies the Old City, surrounded by centuries-old mighty walls with their seven gates through which everything enters or leaves: the Jaffa Gate; the Zion Gate; the Dung Gate; the Lion, or St. Stephen's, Gate; Herod's Gate; the Damascus Gate; and the New Gate.

There is an eighth gate, the Golden Gate, which has been sealed since 1,530 AD, and which is blockaded with Muslim graves. It is said that it is sited over the Closed Gate of the First Temple, and is the entrance through which the Jews believe their Messiah, according to the prophecy in Ezekiel's vision, as recounted in Ezekiel 44:1-3, will pass.

I entered the Old City through the Jaffa, or Pilgrim, Gate on a Friday afternoon.

I was on foot, as all self-respecting pilgrims should be, but carrying rather more luggage than those of the early centuries AD, who traversed whole countries with nothing extra whatsoever. They stepped out in faith, following literally Jesus' instruction to his first disciples when he sent them out to preach the Kingdom of God.

He told them:

'Take nothing for the journey
– no staff, no bag, no bread,
no money, no extra tunic.'
(Luke 9:3)

My comparatively large amount of luggage (anything is a lot compared with nothing at all) was a stark commentary on how far I still had to go in this respect.

Beyond the gate the square teems with life.

To the right tower the great walls of the 16th century Citadel, its cream coloured Jerusalem stone glowing gold in the setting sun. The Citadel embraces Herodean, Roman, Byzantine, Muslim, Mameluke and Ottoman ruins. It was to be one of my favourite places, and where I would watch a magical midnight sound and light presentation of Jerusalem's history.

Ahead is the entrance to the Souk, its dark, narrow, cobbled, stepped walkways lined on either side with stalls selling every conceivable item, from exotic clothes and jewellery to vine leaves. Entering the Souk is like entering a time warp. Little has changed in the many hundreds of years Arabs have traded here. Myriad colours, items for sale, aromas from incense to coffee, and people, compete for your attention.

A blind man squats at the side of one narrow street in the Souk, selling brushes. His head is cocked to one side listening attentively to the waves of sound flowing around him, identifying what is happening and responding accordingly.

I thought of blind Bartimaeus, whose story is told in Mark 10:46, and his reaction when he heard the noise of the crowd as Jesus was passing by. Was this man, too, listening for he-knew-not-what but kept hoping, nevertheless, that he would know it and recognise it when it happened?

At the far end of the narrow tiled streets, I stepped through a small gate into the total contrast of the Temple Mount: an enormous open area full of ancient creamy columns and archways, the sun glittering from the stonework until my eyes ached with the brilliant light.

Dominating it all, the great mosaic walls and golden Dome of the Rock, and the Al Aqsa Mosque; two of the most holy places in the world for Muslims.

Nearby, is the Western, or Wailing, Wall; holy ground for Jews. Its crevices contain numerous prayers left by Jews, who pray there constantly, but especially on Friday evenings, the beginning of Shabbatt.

On this day, at this time, whole families come; there are dancing processions, and social and prayer times. There is a strict division as to where men and women may pray, and a barrier between, but which the young children may cross to and fro freely.

Beyond, the land dips into the Valley of Kidron outside the city walls, then rises again to become the Mount of Olives, a favourite place for Jesus. I sat in some gardens on the Mount and looked back at the walled city, as Jesus must have done so often. Did his throat, too, catch with the seemingly pure beauty of it all?

I re-entered the Old City through St. Stephens Gate, and

began to walk the Via Dolorosa: the Way of Jesus' last journey carrying his Cross.

The deep, resonant and sonorous notes of bells drew me towards the Church of the Holy Sepulchre, one of Christianity's most holy places, and where stark, bare, ancient, underground chapels of rugged rough stone contrast with the highly decorated and ornate upper areas.

As I entered the great building I heard the call to prayer of the Muezzins from the various minarets joining with the bells' proclamation. Each morning of my time in Jerusalem I was to awaken at 4.00 am to this wonderful inter-faith mingling, when the sounds of the first calls and the pealing of the bells rolled together across the city.

The sound of the other's summons to worship is abhorrent to so many, and not only in this place. But, I wondered, how does God hear it?

> Pray not for Arab or Jew,
> for Palestinian or Israeli.
> Pray rather for ourselves
> that we might not divide them
> in our prayers
> but keep them both
> together in our hearts.
> (The prayer of a Palestinian Christian)

I wondered, too whether, despite the numerous churches, synagogues and mosques, does God struggle to make himself heard and felt here?

Jerusalem is, potentially, the heavenly city: the City of Peace.

The last sentence of the Book of the Prophet Ezekiel declared in the 4th century BC: 'The name of the city in future must be "Yahweh-is-there" (Ezekiel 48:35b). The Hebrew 'Yahweh-sham' – 'God-is-there' – suggests Jerusalem.

Its present reality, though, is that it is a city divided and fragmented by the hate, fear, suspicion and injustice, that has always permeated its life: in fact, in many ways, it is just like any other city in the world, with the same problems and preoccupations. God is not always visible, by any means.

It is so tempting to idealise an earthly place, person or thing, and to make that our God. We are all born to worship, and if we don't worship God, we will worship someone, or something, else.

We so need Jerusalem to be perfect, to embody all our longing for a heavenly place here on earth. And, when we find it is not, it is easy to feel disillusioned. However, like every other place in the world, it is shot through with the potential to be the heavenly city of the future. Yahweh-sham, not only in Jerusalem, but everywhere.

On the night before Auschwitz Remembrance Day, as I and others watched the sound and light presentation of Jewish history within the walls of the Citadel, outside the dark sky was lit up by the probing beams of searchlights sweeping the sky. The past and the present were tellingly juxtaposed into a stark parable of the reality of modern-day Israel.

Carved into my mind and heart as well are the many gentle kindnesses and spontaneous generosities I received from Jews, Muslims and Christians.

The elderly Orthodox Rabbi, a noted and much respected scholar and intellectual, who waited in the hot midday sun to ensure that I did not get lost when I first visited him; and the Jewish couple who could not do enough to help, offering to drive me wherever I wanted to go, and placing themselves at my service.

The Arab stall holder in the Souk who would insist on giving me an extra twenty or thirty per cent of exotic dried fruit each time I bought from his stall; and the young Muslim couple who were there when much needed in one particular situation.

The Palestinian Anglican priest, soon to be consecrated Anglican Bishop-Elect in Jerusalem, who gave much of his time to patiently answering my many questions, sharing his reflections and discussing many issues, and who, in parting, told me to remember that the living stones are much more important than the holy stones.

Through these people, and so many others, I received so many blessings.

It is through the life, the death and the resurrection of the Jesus who walked this Land of the Holy, and who now walks the face of the earth in all his many guises, that, whether named or unnamed, each situation is shot through with the potential of his presence, and so hope is woven into every situation, however hopeless it may apparently seem.

The Book of the Prophet Zechariah speaks of how the spiritual and the temporal powers will be closely associated in the messianic age (Zechariah 4), in fulfilment of the prophecy in Jeremiah:

'Look, the days are coming,' Yahweh declares,
'when I shall fulfil the promise of happiness I made to
the House of Israel and the House of Judah:

'"In those days and in that time,
I shall make an upright Branch grow for David,
who will do what is just and upright in the country.
In those days Judah will triumph and Israel live in safety.
And this is the name the city will be called:
Yahweh-is-our-Saving-Justice."'
(Jeremiah 33:14-16)

And so there is also much hope here amongst the hopelessness: in the bravery and the stubborn courageousness of Jewish and Palestinian leaders who insist on pursuing the way of peace, despite much opposition from both sides and much pressure to leave the negotiating table – as well as amongst many ordinary, anonymous people, on both sides, who are prepared to pay the costly price of walking the Christ-path of Shalom.

YAD VASHEM

I will give in my house and within my walls a place and a name.

Set amongst trees in the New City is Yad Vashem, Jerusalem's memorial to Auschwitz and the Holocaust.

At the entrance stands the statue of a silently-screaming mother, holding out her dead child that lies in her arms and yet, at the same time, pulling it back protectively to her breast.

A succession of buildings house harrowing pictures, descriptions, video-films and other memorabilia. The Hall of Names houses the list of names of all known Holocaust victims in a vast line of shelving many rows high.

Walkways are planted with rosebushes and underneath each is a name plaque. One avenue is dedicated in honour of the memory of the 'Righteous Gentiles' who risked their own lives in order to save Jews from death, and so fulfilling the ancient Talmudic precept that whoever saves a life saves the whole of creation.

Statues, and carvings of whole groups of people, some made from twisted metal, some torn from stone, act as silent witnesses to suffering – surprising you and confronting you as you round a corner or a bush or a tree. At these points beauty and pain are graphically juxtaposed in a raw parable of life.

A railway track and a single truck are sited on a hill overlooking Jerusalem; reminder of how bodies were transported to the furnaces.

At the far end of Yad Vashem is the Children's Memorial.

At the entrance, as is the Jewish custom of linking oneself to the people remembered, small stones are piled high on a horizontal metal truck wheel mounted on a plinth.

Inside it is pitch-black, except for myriads of little lights that surround you whichever way you look, whichever way you turn: to the front, to the back, to the side, up, down – everywhere.

You get the sense that you have stepped beyond time and into eternity.

Your companions are the one and a half million children who were murdered in the Holocaust, each represented by one of these shining stars.

Every hour of every day, every day of every year, the rollcall of their names, their ages, and where they lived, is played continually into the otherwise deep, dark silence.

I stayed a long time in there. People came and went around me. But I was reluctant to leave.

Gassed or burned to death, these children were now beyond all pain and agony and, I was sure, in the loving and eternal presence of their heavenly Father.

And I, in their innocent company, felt taken closer to him too.

I had come away from Auschwitz in Poland, asking many of the timeless questions with a new intensity:

– about a God who cannot/will not intervene.
– about the efficacy of prayer.
– about the basic goodness/evil in humankind: which dominates?
– about individual responsibility.
– about forgiveness and its limits – even for God?
– and many others.

But I had come away with answers too.

For me, as a Christian, it was in the worst places that the Cross had seemed most firmly planted: how wonderful is the knowledge that I have those unburnable and eternal pieces of wood to cling to, whatever the situation or the circumstance.

For me as a Christian, the suffering of Christ crucified and the suffering of the inmates of Auschwitz and Birkenau are as intimately intertwined as are the threads of Jesus' seamless garment.

It is said that the birds don't sing at Auschwitz, but I heard a bird sing; a very plain, ordinary, song – yet bird-song, nevertheless.

And, between the huts, I saw that grass was beginning to grow; coarse and rather brown – yet grass, nevertheless.

It is as if even this place of despair and death is struggling to come to birth.

As if God is calling even these shattered fragments to him to be redeemed, and renewed, and to be made whole.

In February 1995,
at the Fiftieth Anniversary Remembrance Ceremony
in Auschwitz,
the newspapers reported that Elie Wiesel prayed:

'God have no mercy on this place.'

His agonized and despairing prayer
must reflect countless others,
each of them patiently and tenderly gathered up
together with the shattered fragments
that is the suffering of Auschwitz,
by God the Healer:

'For it is the will of the Father that nothing be lost.'
(See John 6:39)

An Easter Prayer

Father –
on that joyful morning
you called out your Son.

Jesus –
on that joyful morning
you burst out from the Tomb
that embraced you.

Nothing
could contain the
energy of your New Life
released from all limitations
to fill the world.

All Creation joined in the shout of praise –
and continues to do so
each Easter morn.
The pent-up energy of the earth
overflows in an abundance of colour
that dazzles the eye and quickens the heart.

Birds sing out the new-born hope.

Butterflies celebrate the re-birth
from the confining
but transforming
chrysalis with a dance of creation
from flower to flower.

Risen Lord –
send me out
in the power of the
Holy Spirit
to proclaim your Easter message
of victory over sin and death and
of Love and Peace.

Amen.

WE ARE ONE

In the beginning, God created heaven and earth.
(Genesis 1:1)

Scientists generally agree that the universe was formed in a Big Bang. But they have long been looking for a unified field theory: the basic 'ingredient' behind all of Creation.

Father, may they be one, as we are one.
(John 17:22b)

Science and spirituality are usually thought of as irreconcilable opposites. But both teach that there is an intimate dynamic and inter-relationship between everyone and everything in the world; that the billions of cells that form each one of us are co-ordinated and linked with every other particle in the universe.

Humans, flowers, trees, rocks, birds, angels, animals and insects; all are one.

It is said that, when a butterfly flutters its wings in the Amazon, a storm is caused over the Russian Steppes. Or, as a very well-known Christian writer on spirituality put it: 'When a baby throws its rattle out of its pram, the heavens rock.' (13)

So, we can never know the possibly cataclysmic effect of the smallest of our actions. In our fiercely individualistic world many of us have mislaid our sense of belonging to, and responsibility for, all of Creation.

It is when we lose our sense of corporate identity that we lose our sense of who we are as individuals.

Yet it is our sense of ourselves as unique and precious, but still an intimate part of a wider community, that gives us our humanity.

Paradoxically though, it is only when we lose ourselves in the needs, and the love, of others that we discover who we really are. This is what Jesus was saying when he declared, 'Those who lose their life for my sake will find it.'

Jesus literally lost his life for our sakes, in order that we may find our way back to God.

Now he draws us into union with himself, with the Father and with the Holy Spirit, to join in the Trinity's dance of unity throughout eternity.

God is the lead dancer and the soul is the partner completely attuned to the rhythm and patterns set by the partner. She does not lead, but neither does she hang limp like a sack of potatoes.
(Thomas Merton, Cistercian monk, mystic, writer and poet)

Jesus' prayer at his last earthly meal with his disciples:
'Father, may they be one, as we are one.
With me in them and you in me,
may they be so perfected in unity
that the world will recognise that
it was you who sent me,
and that you have loved them
as you have loved me.'
(John 17:23)

Scientists say that a theory of quantum gravity would be a theory of everything.

However, even after it is discovered, it would still be a long time before all the consequences were found.

Even when they have discovered a theory of everything, it still would not answer the truly important questions of why we are here, or how we are to solve such problems as how to feed the starving people of the world.

So, would we really be any the wiser?

If it has not taught us how to care better for our fellow human beings, our sisters and brothers, we will be just as fragmented as before.

Science needs a spiritual dimension to its thinking to root it in reality and to give it humanity.

It was Jerusalem Day, when the city celebrated its thousands of years of history with parades, music, concerts, dancing, firework displays – and much honking of car horns, a favourite Israeli pastime.

I sat in one of my favourite cafés, run by Armenian Christians, looking out at the square in front of the Citadel, and watching the crowds of young people making their way to the Wailing, or Western, Wall. There was much high spirits and excited anticipation amongst them.

Suddenly, near the doorway, stood a familiar figure. It was the Palestinian beggar who frequented that area, gesticulating with the staff in his hand, and talking loudly.

The owner of the café appeared, bearing a large cup of freshly-squeezed fruit juice and pitta bread stuffed to the brim with fresh salad and meat, which he carried reverently to the beggar. It was all done quietly and discreetly, and with perfect courtesy, as if the owner of the café felt privileged to have the opportunity to serve the beggar.

Some time later, as I left the Old City for the New, I saw another beggar, blind and crouching at the roadside.

A group of young people, aged about twelve years, who were walking in front of me, laughing and joking, stopped. Each felt in their pockets, then placed money respectfully into the open palm of the beggar. Each, as he or she did so, said a word of blessing, before continuing on their way.

Some images of unity:

Trinitarian Quarks: It seems a generally accepted scientific theory at present that the basic building-blocks of everything are quarks and leptons. Quarks gather in tight groups of three. They cannot bear to be alone: you never find an individual quark.

The Dalegura tribe of Australian aborigines took turns to carry a woman, disabled from birth, on their backs until she died naturally at the age of sixty-six years. They did this, because it is their tradition never to desert the sick.

The Salt Doll journeyed for thousands of miles over land until it finally came to the sea. It was fascinated by this strange moving mass, quite unlike anything it had ever seen before.

'Who are you?' the salt girl said to the sea.

The sea smilingly replied, 'Come in and see.'

So the salt doll waded into the sea. The further it walked into the sea the more it dissolved, until there was only very little of it left. Before that last bit dissolved, the doll exclaimed in wonder, 'Now I know who I am!' (14)

There is an African proverb: 'If the foot gets a thorn in it, the whole body must stoop to pull it out.' And St. Paul wrote from Ephesus to the Corinthians, 'If one part (of the body) is hurt, all the parts share its pain. As it is, God has put all the separate parts into the body as he chose. The parts are many, but the body is one. Now Christ's body is yourselves, each of you with a part to play in the whole.' (1 Corinthians 12:26a, 18, 20, 27)

We are all needed. Each one of us is an important, precious and unique part of God's plan, and to whom he has assigned particular tasks and gifts: as the Parable of the Talents reminds us. (Luke 19:11f.)

Like a jigsaw puzzle there are many pieces but, if even one tiny piece is missing, the picture will be incomplete.

RE-CREATION

Send out your breath and life begins; you renew the face of the earth.

Long ago, you laid earth's foundations, the heavens are the work of your hands.

They pass away but you remain, they all wear out like a garment, like outworn clothes you change them.
(Psalms 104:30; 102:25, 26)

. . . for anyone who is in Christ, there is a new creation: the old order is gone and a new being is there to see.
(2 Corinthians 5:17)

After the destruction of Jerusalem, so the story goes, three Rabbis came and stood on a hill overlooking the city. Two wept, but one smiled.

'Why do you smile?' they asked.

'Because,' Rabbi Yeshev replied, 'I remember the prophecies that Jerusalem shall be destroyed and shall be rebuilt.

'Now I have seen the first is true, I know that the second will also come true.'

When the Big Bang occurred, that greatest of all bursts of creative energy, many trillions of fragments were formed: out of the one life came much new life.

Scientists say that the universe is expanding and always has been, ever since that first explosive happening at the beginning of time.

One day, so it is also said, the universe will begin to contract.

Will this be the time, the point at which God finally calls all creation back to himself?

'But you are a chosen people . . .' (1 Peter 2:9) Our tiny planet of Earth is, seemingly, the only piece of matter, or fragment of the universe, able to naturally sustain life such as ours with all its wonder-full diversity.

One theory about the basic building blocks of the universe is that they are not particles but wave-forms which have been given the name 'superstrings'. This is both a very ancient and a very modern idea. This theory holds that billions upon billions of unseen strings pervade the universe, and their different frequencies give rise to all the matter and energy in creation. Certain vibrations also turn into time and space. In this theory, then, primordial sound is the basic building block.

'In the beginning, God created heaven and earth . . . God said, "Let there be light," and there was light.' (Genesis 1:1,3) Over the next six days God continued to speak Creation into existence.

In the third chapter of the Book of Genesis, describing the first sin of humankind and its consequences, a marvellous picture is drawn of the relationship between God the Father and the children he has conceived and created.

In the beginning there is nothing to mar their relationship but, after they have disobeyed God, Adam and Eve hide from him as they are ashamed and frightened by what they have done.

God calls to them because he wants their company to walk with him in the garden he has made for them. When he finds out they have gone against his expressed will he is sad and angry, for they have broken the bond of trust between themselves and him. He decides they will have to earn the right to be in the paradise he has created, so, for now, they must leave. But before they go, like any loving father, he ensures they do not depart unprotected: he makes tunics of skin for them, and clothes them.

God continues to care for, to call to change, to restore and to renew his outworn and fallen creation, and to continue to call it to return to him.

After the Creation stories in Genesis, and all through the Bible, God's continuous care is stressed, without which everything would collapse into nothingness; as well as his absolute right, like a potter, to make of it all what he will:

> Can I not do to you what this potter does? Yes, like clay in the potter's hands so you are in mine. (Jeremiah 18:6)

His co-worker is Jesus Christ.

> And God held in his hand
> A small globe. Look, he said.
> The son looked. Far off,
> As through water, he saw
> A scorched land of fierce
> Colour. The light burned
> There; Crusted buildings
> Cast their shadows: a bright
> Serpent, a river
> Uncoiled itself, radiant
> With slime.

On a bare
Hill a bare tree saddened
The sky. Many people
Held out their thin arms
To it, as though waiting
For a vanished April
To return to its crossed
Boughs. The son watched
Them. Let me go there, he said. (15)

God, who created all things through Christ, has restored his
work, deformed by sin, by recreating it in Christ.

In the beginning was the Word, the Word was with God
and the Word was God . . .
The Word was the real light
that gives light to everyone; he came into the world . . .
To those who accepted him he gave power to become
children of God . . .
(John 1:1, 9, 12a)

So it must have been on Calvary
In the fiercer light of the thorns' halo:
The men standing by and that one lone figure,
The hands bleeding, the mind bruised but calm,
Making such music as lives still.
And no one daring to interrupt
Because it was himself that he played
And closer than all of them the God listened. (16)

So God works in partnership to bring about his new creation.

And we are not to be passive or indifferent bystanders and onlookers in this mightiest of acts.

We, too, have our part to play.

We are called to be co-creators with him, actively involved in bringing about the new creation, the heavenly Jerusalem, upon the earth in whichever situations God places us.

God is not only the Lord of the Universe, but also Giver of the tiny white flower which brings comfort, sustains and heals.

One morning, at a time of very great personal worry, when I felt I had almost reached the end of my ability to cope with the traumatic situation, I went into my garden to pray. Overnight a perfect circular cluster of pure white flowers had appeared where none had ever flowered before. Each tiny flower had four petals, each was beautiful in its perfect simplicity. No one could explain how they came to be there: where they had come from was mystery.

They became a focus of peace for me each day over the following weeks.

Then, one day, the good news for which I had been longing, but for which I had scarcely dared hope. I went into the garden, my heart spilling over with gratitude. The flowers were gone – and have never returned.

> . . . The world in a grain of sand
> And heaven in a wild flower. (17)

LOVE

For this is how God loved the world: he gave his only Son, so that everyone who believes in him may not perish, but may have eternal life.
(John 3:16)

This verse must rate as the most famous in the whole Bible, and as the ultimate example of minimalism.

In just a few words, packed with explosive meaning, is summed up the essence of the Christian message.

It takes a moment to read, but a lifetime to absorb and to understand its implications for each of us and for the world.

'We cannot begin to understand the infinitely large without studying the unimaginably small.' (18)

A drawing of an atom, with its electrons speeding round a nucleus, is remarkably similar to a drawing of the planets revolving around the sun.

An example of a macro-system is the Universe, with its seeming infinity of galaxies. An example of a micro-system is the brain, with its billions of cells and trillions of synapses.

The microcosmic, the infinitely small, always has macrocosmic implications. So, everything is important and has consequences; the smallest happening reverberating throughout the Universe.

Surely only a God of the most amazing and infinite love could be so attentive to all that he has created that he can be both Lord of the Universe and aware of the smallest happening in his Creation.

He is 'the love that moves the sun and the other stars'. (19)

Returning from the Holocaust Remembrance Day event at the Wailing Wall in Jerusalem, held to mark the liberation of the inmates from the death-camps fifty years before, I found a sparrow lying dead upon the ground beside the Zion Gate and just within the walls of the Old City.

> Can you not buy two sparrows for a penny? And yet not one falls to the ground without your Father knowing. Why, every hair on your head has been counted.
> So there is no need to be afraid; you are worth more than many sparrows. (Matthew 10:29-31)

After two miscarriages, and a difficult labour lasting some forty hours, my first child was finally born.

The doctor laid her in my arms. Following that first triumphant cry declaiming her arrival, she was peacefully asleep. I looked in wonder and joy and delighted recognition at the beautiful, heart-shaped face, the skin of which was already a gentle cream and pink. The hair, which was to become a trademark lay, already thick and soft, upon her scalp.

This small person, this heavenly gift, was truly a pinnacle of God's creation.

For nine months I had held her in my womb and, now I held her in my arms, it was like greeting someone I already knew very well.

As I held her, and gazed at her, a wave of love swept through me with the intensity of an electric shock so strong that I really think I could not have sustained it without it consuming me.

It was a momentary glimpse and experience of something of the Father's love for each of us: his children.

Two more miscarriages, and then my son was born: a second miracle, and another of Love's gifts.

A thought transfixed me: for the first time in my life I saw the truth, as it is set into song by so many poets, proclaimed as the final wisdom by so many thinkers.

The truth that love is the ultimate and highest goal to which man can aspire.

Then I grasped the meaning of the greatest secret that human poetry and human thought and belief have to impart: the salvation of man is through love and in love. (20)

In his stunning poem the *Hound of Heaven*, Francis Thompson vividly describes his desperate attempts to escape the clutches of his relentless pursuer:

> I fled Him, down the nights and down the days;
> I fled Him, down the arches of the years;
> I fled Him, down the labyrinthine ways
> Of my own mind . . . (21)

He knows that it is Love that pursues him, but is terrified of the all-embracing demands that Love may make upon him.

Finally, exhausted, he can run no more.

It is only then that he comes to the realisation that the

dark threat was – and had always been – 'the shade of His hand, outstretched caressingly.'

> Were the whole realm of nature mine
> That were an offering far too small,
> Love so amazing, so divine,
> Demands my life,
> My soul,
> My all. (22)

> You fence me in behind and in front;
> you have laid your hand upon me.
> Where shall I go to escape your spirit?
> Where shall I flee from your presence?

> If I speed away on the wings of the dawn;
> if I dwell beyond the ocean,
> even there your right hand will be guiding me,
> your right hand holding me fast.
> (Psalm 139:7, 9, 10)

WHOLENESS

Scientists are currently trying to understand the symmetry and asymmetry of our universe: the essential interdependence and interconnectedness of opposites which holds the universe in being.

'. . . The coincidence of all opposites.'
(Thomas Merton)

Most present scientific theory states that the universe began in a hot Big Bang some fifteen thousand million years ago.

Out of this fireball, matter emerged along with antimatter. Antimatter is a sort of mirror image of matter, but carrying the opposite sign of electric charge, and is antagonistic towards matter which it destroys if it comes into contact with it.

You would expect then that, scarcely before the world had begun, matter and antimatter would have annihilated each other, and our universe as we know it would have died at birth.

Somehow though, in the first moments of time, matter emerged victorious, the antimatter having been annihilated.

Why should this be so? Because, apparently, nature has a tiny inbuilt balance: a tendency for antimatter not to mimick precisely its matter counterpart. And so there is symmetry and asymmetry, an interdependence and interconnectedness of opposites, holding the universe in being.

Two and a half thousand years ago Empedocles, a Greek philosopher, was teaching that the universe is held in tension by discord among the elements. From time to time the motions of the heavens brought about a state of harmony (love). When this happened, like matter flew to like, and the universe was once more resolved into its original elements and so reduced to chaos.

In the 13th century AD, another world-famous writer and poet called Dante wrote of his visionary journey to wholeness, beginning in hell and fragmentation, and ending in paradise. Here, he beholds the Creator – and sees the universe, the human and the divine, all joined and one with God.

His story reaches its end, and its beginning, with Dante's own will and desire moving in perfect co-ordination with the love of God.

Seven hundred years later the twentieth-century monk, Thomas Merton, wrote of

The coincidence of all opposites:
a fusion of freedom and unfreedom,
being and unbeing,
life and death,
I and non-I,
yes and no,
human and God.
We must contain all divided worlds in ourselves.

Thomas Merton faced all the opposites and tensions within his own self and let them converge, as he sought to live the life of a hermit and yet still respond authentically to a world which clamoured for his wisdom and his insight.

For both Thomas Merton and Dante Alighieri, wholeness is everything finally woven together: just as Christ's seamless garment – so finely woven that warp and weft could not be distinguished – represents his life and death and resurrection.

The lover knocked at the door of his Beloved.

'Who knocks?' said the Beloved from within.

'It is I,' said the lover.

'Then go away. This house will not hold you and me.'

The rejected lover went away into the desert. There he meditated for months on end, pondering the words of the Beloved.

Finally, he returned and knocked at the door again.

'Who knocks?'

'It is you.'

The door immediately opened. (23)

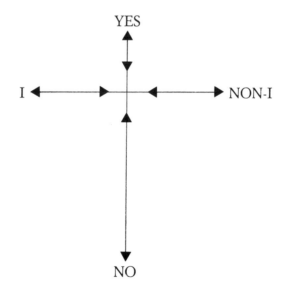

THE COINCIDENCE OF ALL OPPOSITES

The Church of the Holy Sepulchre in Jerusalem is considered one of the most holy places on earth.

In the middle of the Church of the Holy Sepulchre is the Katholikon.

In the centre of the Katholikon is a marble hemisphere which, according to ancient Christian tradition, represents the Navel, or centre, of the world.

Nearby, is the Chapel of the Holy Sepulchre, thought by many Christians to be the place where Jesus' body was laid after being taken down from the Cross. This is the still point at the eye of the storm of wrangling and bickering, by the seven different denominations who minister in this church, over who has prime claim to being there.

Each group hesitates to assist, and is eager to hinder, the others.

'When one denomination has a celebration, the others have a cleaning day,' as one local Christian wryly observed.

Greater than all the petty wrangling though, surrounding it and embracing it, permeating and transforming it – yet also standing out and beyond it – is the eternal presence and peace of God which is felt in the church despite all that human frailty can do to deny it.

I discovered the following song on an old record of Paul Robeson, the gentle black giant with a passion for social and racial justice, who was vilified and exiled from the country of his birth for his views.

His deep, rich and tender voice singing this song of love, constancy and commitment has an eternal quality about it that makes me imagine it as a dialogue between God the Lover and his beloved.

Where you go
my heart shall follow after,
there's no road
you can escape me by;
joy or woe
your sorrow and your laughter
I will share with you
until you die.

There's a new
magic in the air,
magic everywhere,
magic in the breeze
among the trees:
It is You.
Ever since You came
nothing is the same;
just to speak Your Name
sets me all aflame.
Ever since I fell
underneath Your spell
I dream of You:
it is You!

Where you go
my heart shall follow after,
there's no road
you can escape me by;
joy or woe
your sorrow and your laughter
I will share with you
until you die.

LIGHT

I am the light of the world. Anyone who follows me will not be walking in the dark, but will have the light of life.
(John 8:12)

Then Jesus laid his hands on the man's eyes again and he saw clearly: he was cured, and he could see everything plainly and distinctly. (Mark 8:25)

Cosmologists claim to be able to construct models of the first few minutes of the universe's life, apart from the first few microseconds. However, as yet, they cannot get further as they are met with an opaqueness beyond which they cannot penetrate.

One latest theory is that there were fields of potentiality before the Big Bang and that, when energy was poured onto these electronic fields, matter was created: potentiality became actuality.

However, where the original energy came from scientists don't know: what they are exploring before the Big Bang is no-thing.

Spiritual writers down the ages have spoken of God as screened by a dark cloud of unknowing, a brilliant blackness, a deep and dazzling darkness; a God of no-thing, because he is beyond our limited powers of perception and description.

So, how can we know him if he is a God of no-thing?

The miracle is as recounted in John's Gospel:

No one has ever seen God,
it is the only Son, Jesus Christ,
who is close to the Father's heart,
who has made him known.
(John 1:17, 18)

And once, as Jesus was teaching in the Temple in Jerusalem, he cried out,

'. . . He who sent me is true;
you do not know him, but I know him,
because I have my being in him
and it was he who sent me.'
(John 7:28, 29)

A short distance outside the Damascus Gate, along the Nablus road in the Arab Quarter, is the Garden Tomb.

This rock-hewn tomb was discovered some one hundred years ago by an Englishman who had been previously impressed by the resemblance of the nearby rockface to a skull.

'They brought Jesus to the place called Golgotha, which means the place of the skull . . . Then they crucified him.' (Mark 15:22, 24a)

It is thought by a number of people, and an interesting case been made, that this is in fact the place where Jesus' body was placed after the Crucifixion, and not the Holy Sepulchre.

It is good for us to have our beliefs challenged in this way, by more than one shrine claiming to be the authentic place where one or another religious event happened, for it reminds us that it is the event that we remember and venerate, and not the memorial and artefacts that mark the spot. A shrine should be like an ikon, a way of drawing us deeper into the mystery it represents. In Israel, you have plenty of opportunity to put this philosophy into practice.

Unlike the Holy Sepulchre, there are no competitive religious factions at the Garden Tomb. The gardens are beautiful and lovingly tended, and an air of peace and tranquillity pervades the place. The dark entrance of the Tomb contrasts starkly with the surrounding white stone of the hillside out of which it is hewn.

I sat on a stone step, a short distance from the entrance, as dawn stained the sky and the stone around the Tomb a deep crimson.

All was quiet and still.

A young man was already watering some flowerbeds nearby, before it became too hot. It was easy to imagine a weeping Mary, half-blinded by tears, turning from the Tomb and, in the half-light, mistaking Jesus for a gardener such as this young man.

As the sun climbed higher the whole area began to shimmer with brighter and brighter light, which coloured the white stones until they seemed to be aflame.

The dark entrance of the Tomb was even blacker and more mysterious by contrast: a deep and dazzling darkness, a brilliant blackness at the very centre, the very heart, of the light.

I was both awed by and inexorably drawn to it.

It was the kind of evening when, the air oppressive with imminent thunderstorms, you cannot settle to anything – and so I went for a walk by the sea.

It was a starless, rain-flecked night and I was, it seemed, the only one foolish enough to be out. Great, black clouds banked heavily overhead and toward the horizon. I stood looking out across the water, which was curiously flat and quiet under the active sky.

Suddenly, everything stilled, as if Creation had caught its breath.

Over the sea, a perfect double rainbow formed, with each

of the ends dipping into the waters beneath. In between the arcs of red, orange, yellow, green, blue, indigo and violet – each glowing colour clearly defined – the sky was radiant with light; its brilliance intensified by the blackness of the clouds beyond the bows.

It was awesome in its perfection.

It was as if God was creating for the sheer joy of it, just because he loved to create and to be surrounded by beauty.

And I, as an imperfect human being who could have felt like an intruder inadvertently stumbling upon some private, so ancient and yet so new, ritual being enacted, felt God was happy to have me there. Not because I deserved it, but because he is a God of generosity and love, whose pleasure it is to share all that he has made – and part of which he had drawn together for this miraculous manifestation of his glory and promise.

My love loves me,
And oh! the wonders I see:
A rainbow shines in my window,
My love loves me.
(Folk Song)

And God said, 'This is the sign of the covenant I am making between me and you and every living creature with you, a covenant for all generations to come: I have set my rainbow in the clouds, and it will be the sign of the covenant between me and the earth. When I bring clouds over the earth and the rainbow appears in the clouds, I will remember my covenant between me and you and all the creatures of every living kind.'
(Genesis 9:12-16)

A Covenant Prayer

Take, Lord, and receive
All my liberty,
My memory,
My understanding,
My entire will.
All that I have and possess,
Everything is yours:
You gave it all to me,
And to you I now return it.
So now take me, Lord,
And do what you want with me;
Only give me your grace
And your love –
And that will be enough for me.
(St. Ignatius of Loyola)

THE JERUSALEM OF
THE FUTURE

THE HEAVENLY JERUSALEM

Then I saw a new heaven and a new earth; the first heaven and the first earth had disappeared now, and there was no longer any sea. I saw the holy city, the new Jerusalem, coming down out of heaven from God, prepared as a bride dressed for her husband.

Then I heard a loud voice call from the throne, 'Look, here God lives among human-beings. He will make his home among them; they will be his people, and he will be their God, God-with-them.

'He will wipe all tears from their eyes; there will be no more death, and no more mourning or sadness or pain. The world of the past has gone.'

Then the One sitting on the throne spoke.

'Look, I am making the whole of creation new.

'Write this. What I am saying is trustworthy and will come true.' Then he said to me, 'It has already happened. I am the Alpha and the Omega, the Beginning and the End.

'I will give water from the well of life free to anybody who is thirsty; anyone who proves victorious will inherit these things; and I will be their God, and they shall be my people.'
(Revelation 21:1-7)

EPILOGUE

SHALOM

In John's Gospel we read how, after Jesus had appeared to Mary Magdalene, he appeared twice more to his disciples, in the rooms in which they were gathered behind locked doors.

Each time, the first thing he says is,

'Peace be with you.'
(John 20:19-29)

Later on, Jesus revealed himself again to the disciples. It was by the Sea of Tiberias, and it happened like this . . .

Simon Peter, Thomas called the Twin, Nathaniel from Cana in Galilee, the sons of Zebedee and two more of his disciples were together. Simon Peter said, 'I'm going fishing.' They replied, 'We'll come with you.' They went out and got into the boat but caught nothing that night.

When it was already light, there stood Jesus on the shore, though the disciples did not realise that it was Jesus. Jesus called out, 'Haven't you caught anything, friends?' And when they answered, 'No,' he said, 'Throw the net out to starboard and you'll find something.' So they threw the net out and could not haul it in because of the quantity of fish.

The disciple whom Jesus loved said to Peter, 'It is the Lord.' Simon Peter tied his outer garment round him (for he had nothing on) and jumped into the water. The other disciples came on in the boat, towing the net with the fish; they were only about a hundred yards from land.

As soon as they came ashore they saw that there was some bread there and a charcoal fire with fish cooking on it. Jesus said, 'Bring some of the fish you have just caught.'

Simon Peter went aboard and dragged the net ashore, full of big fish, one hundred and fifty-three of them; and in spite of there being so many the net was not broken.

Jesus said to them, 'Come and have breakfast.' None of the disciples was bold enough to ask, 'Who are you?' They knew quite well it was the Lord. Jesus then stepped forward, took the bread and gave it to them, and the same with the fish. This was the third time that Jesus revealed himself to the disciples after rising from the dead.

When they had eaten, Jesus said to Simon Peter, 'Simon son of John, do you love me more than these others do?' He answered, 'Yes, Lord, you know I love you.' Jesus said to him, 'Feed my lambs.'

A second time he said to him, 'Simon son of John, do you love me?' He replied, 'Yes, Lord, you know that I love you.' Jesus said to him, 'Look after my sheep.'

Then he said to him a third time, 'Simon son of John, do you love me?' Peter was hurt that he asked him a third time, 'Do you love me?' and said, 'Lord, you know everything; you know I love you.'

Jesus said to him, 'Feed my sheep.'

(John 21:1-17)

I arrived, weary and footsore, at a place called Tabgha on the shore of the Sea of Tiberias. It was three o'clock in the afternoon, and I had been walking all day in the hot sun, which now glistened and sparkled on the water which had been witness to so many marvellous and miraculous events.

Here stands what is, for me, the most beautiful church in the whole of Israel: the Church of the Primacy of Peter.

It is tiny. A large rock fills most of the floorspace, symbol of the leadership Jesus conferred upon Peter:

> ... I now say to you:
> You are Peter
> and on this rock
> I will build my community.
> (Matthew 16:18)

There is a stillness and a deep peace in the utter simplicity of the place. Birds fly in and out of the open door, and nest above the altar. Flowers grow up between cracks in the stone floor.

This tiny chapel sits close beside the water's edge.

On its seaward side is another rock upon which, it is said, Jesus stood and called out to the disciples in their boat, telling them where to cast their nets.

I took off my shoes – for this is holy ground – and stood in the cool, refreshing water near to the rock. Many fish, of varying size, were conspicuous in the crystal-clear sea.

The peace and the beauty of it all seeped into me, until I felt it pervade and fill my whole being.

It was a long time before I reluctantly left the sea, dried my feet, and replaced my shoes in preparation for moving on – for my journeying is not yet done . . .

Before I left England to journey to Israel, I was given the following prayer by someone who himself had travelled to Jerusalem some years previously: walking there in the cause of justice and of peace.

It accompanied me throughout my journeying, which included close encounters with a bomb scare, a car bomb, a Molotov Cocktail, and other eventful happenings.

This powerful and beautiful prayer was a constant blessing as it reminded me of a Trinity who watches continually over each one of us and who longs, and seeks, to weave its love and its peace into the very fabric of our minds and our hearts and our lives.

Now I offer it to you. May it keep you safe in your journeyings.

The weaving of peace be thine
Peace around thy soul entwine
Peace of the Father flowing free
Peace of the Son hovering over thee
Peace of the Spirit for thee, and me
Peace of the one
Peace of the three
A weaving of peace be upon thee.
(A Celtic Prayer)

REFERENCES

No.	Page	
1	13	Elie Wiesel: *Souls on Fire & Somewhere a Master* pp. 93/4, Penguin 1984.
2	13	Dante: *The Divine Comedy 1. Hell* from the *Oxford Dictionary of Quotations, alt.*
3	15	Emil Faekenheim: *To Mend the World* p. 323.
4	16	Elie Wiesel: *Night* p. 10, Penguin 1981.
5	17	Source unknown.
6	28	Dante: *The Divine Comedy 1. Hell* p. 89 Trans. by D. L. Sayers, Penguin 1949.
7	35	Michael Walker: *In 'The Shade of His Hand'* Ed. by M. Hollings and E. Gullick, Mayhew-McCrimmon 1973.
8	45	Viktor Frankl: *Man's Search for Meaning,* Beacon Press, Boston.
9	49	David L. Fleming S.J.: *A Contemporary Reading of the Spiritual Exercises,* The Institute of Jesuit Sources, St Lewis, 1987.
10	51	Dante: *The Divine Comedy 1. Hell* p. 143 Penguin 1949.
11	58	Anon.: *Prayers of the Martyrs* Comp. and Trans. D. W. H. Arnold p. 73, Zondervan Publishing House.

12	68	Fred Kaan: *Hymns for Today* p. 28.
13	87	G. W. Hughes S.J.: *God of Surprises* p. 63 Darton, Longman and Todd 1985.
14	90	A. de Mello S.J: *The Song of the Bird* p. 124 Gujarat Sahitya Prakash, India 1983.
15	95	R. S. Thomas: *The Coming, Later Poems 1972-82,* Macmillan 1984.
16	95	R. S. Thomas: *The Musician Selected Poems 1946-68,* Macmillan 1984.
17	96	W. Blake: *Auguries of Innocence, The London Book of Eng. Verse* Sel. by H. Read & B. Dobree.
18	97	N. Henbest: *The Exploding Universe* p. 92f. Marshal Cavendish 1979.
19	98	Dante: *The Divine Comedy. 3: Paradise* Penguin 1962 Trans. D. L. Sayers and B. Reynolds.
20	99	Viktor Frankl: *Man's Search for Meaning,* Beacon Press, Boston.
21	99	F. Thompson: *The Hound of Heaven* in *The London Book of English Verse* Eyre & Spottiswode 1949.
22	100	I. Watts: *When I survey . . .* in *Hymns A. & M Rev.*
23	103	A. de Mello S.J.: *Who am I?* in *The Song of the Bird* p. 126, 1983.

If unacknowledged, all other meditations, poems and reflections are the work of the author.